1993

THE ALHAZAI
OF MARADI

An *Alhaji* of Maradi

THE ALHAZAI
OF MARADI
Traditional Hausa Merchants in a Changing Sahelian City

Emmanuel Grégoire

edited and translated by
Benjamin H. Hardy

Lynne Rienner Publishers • Boulder & London

Published in the United States of America in 1992 by
Lynne Rienner Publishers, Inc.
1800 30th Street, Boulder, Colorado 80301

and in the United Kingdom by
Lynne Rienner Publishers, Inc.
3 Henrietta Street, Covent Garden, London WC2E 8LU

First published in France by Editions de l'ORSTOM as
*Les Alhazai de Maradi (Niger): Histoire d'un groupe de
riches marchands sahéliens.* © 1986 by ORSTOM

Photo credit: pp. ii, 85–89—Emmanuel Grégoire

Library of Congress Cataloging-in-Publication Data
Grégoire, Emmanuel, 1951–
    [Alhazai de Maradi, Niger. English]
    The Alhazai of Maradi : traditional Hausa merchants in a changing
Sahelian city / Emmanuel Grégoire; translated and edited by
Benjamin H. Hardy.
      p. cm.
    Translation of: Les Alhazai de Maradi, Niger.
    Includes bibliographical references and index.
    ISBN 1-55587-278-6 (alk. paper)
    1. Merchants—Niger—Maradi—History. 2. Maradi (Niger)—
Commerce—History. 3. Maradi (Niger)—Economic conditions.
I. Hardy, Benjamin H. II. Title.
HF3924.Z9M37413 1992   91-35195
381'.1'089937--dc20   CIP

British Cataloguing in Publication Data
A Cataloguing in Publication record for this book
is available from the British Library.

Printed and bound in the United States of America

To my father
–*E. G.*

For my sons: Benjamin, Brian, Richard, William
–*B. H. H.*

Contents

Illustrations

TABLES

Preface to the
English-Language Edition

Since the first appearance of this study, published in France by ORSTOM in
1986, a number of important economic and political events in Niger and in
neighboring Nigeria have affected the activities of the *Alhazai* who operate in
and from Maradi. It appears worthwhile, therefore, to review them briefly for
the reader in order to situate the work that follows within a meaningful context of recent history.

   In Niger, the long illness of President Seyni Kountché (ending with his
death in November 1987) and his succession by General Ali Saibou were the
most important political events. The transfer of power occurred without
difficulty or conflict, largely because President Saibou quickly showed
himself to be more affable and less authoritarian than his predecessor. In May
1989 the Conseil Militaire Suprême was dissolved and replaced by a
constitutional one-party state, whose sole legal political organization was the
Mouvement National pour la Société de Développement (MNSD). That
party's highest organ, the Conseil Supérieur d'Orientation Nationale
(CSON), controls the government; it counts civilians as well as military
officers among its members. More recently, the wave of support for
democratic government that swept Africa during 1990 and 1991 arrived in
Niger as well. General Ali Saibou, bowing to pressure from Niger's urban
masses, accepted the principle of multiparty politics and legalized the creation
of new parties, which immediately proliferated. He then invited Nigerien
notables, including leaders of the new parties, to participate in a national
convention (held in July 1991) to create new, more democratic political and
governmental institutions. Although these measures demonstrate a certain
openness on the part of the regime, the soldiers nevertheless show little
readiness to abandon to civilians the power they have held since 1974.

   In Nigeria, by contrast, General Ibrahim Babangida, who has been in
power since August 1985, has committed himself to turn the reins of
government back to civilians in October 1992. In order to escape the ethnic
and religious rivalries that have characterized Nigerian politics in the past,
President Babangida has adopted a two-party system similar to those in Great
Britain and the United States. For the 1992 elections, the Social Democratic
Party and the National Republican Convention will confront each other.

   Since 1987 economic conditions in the two countries have also changed markedly. Niger has experienced especially difficult conditions: agriculture has been extremely vulnerable to climatic variations, and uranium, the country's principal export-revenue earner, no longer produces substantial revenues because world demand, and consequently world prices, have fallen sharply. The resulting financial crisis forced Niger to undertake rigorous measures, including a structural adjustment program worked out with the World Bank. The program featured steps to bring balance-of-payments and national budget deficits under control and to stimulate economic growth. Although the benefits of structural adjustment take a long time to appear, the social costs (staff reductions and salary arrears especially) are felt immediately; as a result, in its second-phase structural adjustment program the government included special projects to alleviate the suffering.

Nigeria also underwent a structural adjustment program, earning good marks from multilateral institutions such as the International Monetary Fund (IMF) and the World Bank. Initiated in 1986, the Nigerian program focused on strict fiscal and monetary policies, foreign exchange rate reforms (which set in motion successive devaluations of Nigeria's currency, the naira), and measures to liberalize foreign trade, including elimination of import licenses, reductions in price controls, and abolition of a number of marketing boards. Among these steps, the very steep naira devaluations had the greatest effect on the economy of Niger, which is strongly dependent upon that of its powerful neighbor. For example, trade along the border between the two countries was disrupted: in January 1991 the parallel market rate (which is used for most transactions, the major exception being government business) was 40 naira per 1000 CFA francs (CFA stands for Communauté Financière Africaine), whereas in December 1986 it had been 14.3 naira and in January 1985, 8.6 naira.

Under the circumstances it is not surprising that the *Alhazai* of Maradi, whose activities are so strongly oriented toward trade with Nigeria, no longer flourished as they had in the past, not even those who had survived the naira demonetization decreed by General Mohammed Buhari in April 1984 and the long closing of the land frontiers that accompanied it (lasting until February 1986).* From then on Nigerian clients had far less purchasing power abroad and consequently were no longer as interesting to the *Alhazai*. The economic liberalization policies adopted by the authorities in Lagos (in particular the elimination of import licenses for certain products) rendered obsolete various kinds of fraud between the two countries, although smuggling continued to be profitable for products such as fabrics, cigarettes, alcoholic beverages, and rice. In addition to these difficulties, a sharp reduction in purchasing by the government of Niger affected the *Alhazai*. In sum, it was a very gloomy economic climate for them, though a few still handle substantial amounts of cash.

In time, perhaps, the *Alhazai* will overcome their difficulties and enjoy good years again: as they have often said themselves, the frontier with Nigeria is still there, and the proximity of that giant African market will constitute a source of business for a long time to come. In that sense, they are poised to profit from a competitive advantage inherent in Maradi's geographic location.

A note on Niger's monetary system: Throughout the text that follows, monetary values are typically and naturally given in Niger's currency, the CFA franc. The CFA franc is shared by thirteen nations, seven of them (Benin, Burkina Faso, Côte d'Ivoire, Niger, Mali, Senegal, Togo) composing the Union Monétaire Ouest-Africaine (UMOA), which came into being in 1974. Through UMOA, the French republic provides a stable monetary system to its former colonies in West Africa. The French treasury maintains a UMOA operations account in Paris, governed by a committee dominated by French officials. African member governments have only marginal influence on the parity value of the CFA franc or on the overall stability of the UMOA system. Each member country in the UMOA is technically obliged to repay its capital account obligations to the French treasury, but the French government continues to give de facto grants to Niger and other poor members by repaying their accounts due.

The institution through which UMOA operates in Niger is the Banque Centrale des Etats de l'Afrique de l'Ouest (BCEAO), which was reorganized in 1962 following the independence of its members. The BCEAO regulates the money supply and sets bank rates separately for each member, taking into account the state of the country's economy and its balances with the French treasury. Niger and the other African member countries thus sacrifice sovereignty over their own money and banking in return for a stable exchange rate and a convertible currency.

The parity rate for convertibility of the CFA franc is 50 CFA francs for 1 French franc. This rate has remained unchanged since 1948; it long ago evolved into one of the pillars of Franco-African cooperation. As a result, the value of the CFA franc in comparison with the US dollar has fluctuated with changes in the exchange rates between the French franc and the dollar. In order to give US readers an indication of the values involved in Niger's trade and economic development, we provide market rates, averaged over the year, in this table:

Exchange Rate Value of US$1 in CFA Francs

Year	1983	1984	1985	1986	1987	1988	1989	1990
CFA francs	381	437	449	346	301	298	319	272

Source: IMF, *International Financial Statistics*

As of mid-1991, 1 million CFA francs were worth about US$3,300.

—*E. G.*
—*B. H. H.*

---

[*] Emmanuel Grégoire, "Les chemins de la contrabande: étude de réseaux commerciaux en pays haoussa," forthcoming in *Cahiers d'Etudes Africaines*, 1992.

Translator's Acknowledgments

Dr. Grégoire's perceptive study of Maradi's Hausa merchants first came to my attention at Niamey, Niger, in February 1989, through the thoughtfulness of Mr. Michael Kerst of the US Agency for International Development (USAID). At that time I was a consultant to USAID/Niger on a project to suggest ways the Republic of Niger might revise its policies, laws, and regulations governing foreign trade. *Les Alhazai de Maradi* was an invaluable source of insight into Niger's trade with Nigeria, its economically powerful southern neighbor—not only examining what was traded but how the trade was organized, who conducted it, and what it meant to people on both sides of the border.

As I read Dr. Grégoire's book, I marveled at his ability to communicate complex ideas in simple language. So easy was my comprehension that I often felt his sentences might well have been translated originally from English into French; certainly, I realized, it should be relatively painless to render them from his clear French into English. This was the germ of an effort that has occupied my spare hours ever since, taking far longer than expected because of several visits to other parts of West Africa, but also providing a challenge and considerable satisfaction at finally mastering it. In the process I have found Dr. Grégoire to be a sympathetic partner and friend, whose help has contributed much to the final product; I offer him my thanks. I offer special thanks to Lynne Rienner as well, for her encouragement, but especially for her patience.

—*B. H. H.*

Author's Acknowledgments

I would like to express my appreciation to those who helped me, in France as well as in Niger, with the completion of my doctoral thesis, from which several elements of this book, originally published as *Les Alhazai de Maradi: Histoire d'un groupe de riches marchands sahéliens*, are drawn.

In France, my thanks go first to Professor Jean Koechlin of the University of Bordeaux III, who agreed to direct my work while allowing me great latitude in its realization. In addition, I wish to thank Claude Raynaut, director of research at the Centre National de la Recherche Scientifique, who encouraged me and helped me undertake this study of the city of Maradi, which complements a multiplicity of researches in the bush either by himself or by the University of Bordeaux II team that he leads.

In Niger, I offer warm thanks to the Nigerien authorities, in particular the Institute for Human Sciences Research. At Maradi, my work was facilitated thanks to the help of Mr. Rhony Issufou, former mayor of Maradi; *Alhaji* Omar, then *sarki* of the Planning Service for the Department of Maradi; and Mr. Ousmane Boubakar, then inspector of general revenues. My gratitude goes also to my interviewers, Habou Magagi, veteran interviewer of the Institute for Human Sciences Research, and Oumarou Ibrahim, who while working with me perhaps began a long "career" as an interviewer. I would like to offer special thanks to numerous informants, including several *Alhazai*, who helped me with my investigations.

Finally, my sincere thanks to Dr. Benjamin H. Hardy. On his own initiative, he undertook to translate the edition first published in French by ORSTOM. Throughout what must have been a tedious effort, he remained faithful to the meaning and spirit of the original text. I salute his skill.

—E. G.

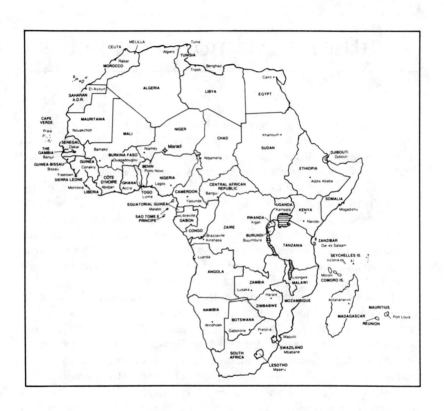

Introduction

Urbanization, although a recent phenomenon, has nonetheless reached all Third World countries and, particularly in the most important cities, has become so rapid and widespread that it overwhelms local social systems. Its impact is not only demographic but also economic, political, moral, and social.

This urban vitality disturbs the equilibrium of traditional societies and sets in motion a new dynamic. It affects a broad range of social groups by introducing profound internal changes, tensions, and disruptions from which emerge new social relationships, often ones similar to those existing in Western nations. The effervescence of new activities makes the city a troubled place, both anticipating the evolution of society and prefiguring its future structure.

This growth of cities often arises from critical problems confronting the population in the surrounding countryside: in many countries of Africa, the Americas, and Asia, the urban explosion is fed by an optimistic rural exodus. To borrow an expression from Richard Gascon, the town offers "a someplace else, where there are abundant opportunities to find work, a chance to live well, and a supportive refuge."[1]

In the course of the past few years, studies of this theme in Africa have multiplied, many of them dealing with large metropolitan areas such as Abidjan, Dakar, Douala, Lomé, and Niamey. The cities of middling importance, where the significance of development lies in the integration of the rural world with modern life, have received less frequent attention. This is regrettable, and one may hope the future will see them studied more systematically. The present study is written with that hope in mind; its purpose is to contribute to the analysis of secondary cities by means of one specifically on Maradi, in the Republic of Niger.

In the Hausa country, and particularly in the area around Maradi, it is impossible to maintain a dualistic analytical schema that contrasts a peasant

1

community fixed in tradition against a "modern" society in the cities, because these have long been the two poles of a single culture, simultaneously rural and mercantile. Town and country are thus so intimately related that one cannot comprehend the recent growth of a place like Maradi without understanding the grave crisis that the rural community has faced ever since severe drought struck the area—and the Sahelian region generally—during the late 1960s and early 1970s.

There is an incessant circular flow of goods and money between town and country. Maradi is the focal point from which these flows radiate, and the local merchants are its center of gravity. Celebrated throughout Niger and known everywhere as *Alhazai* (the singular form is *Alhaji*), they symbolize a new kind of man, steeped in the values of Islam but also in those of merchant capitalism.

In Hausa society, material wealth is closely linked with social status, measured as "a richness in men," or *arzikin mutane* (see Chapter 3). The ways in which material wealth is accumulated, employed, and distributed have much to do with whether a particular merchant is also "rich in men." The most successful Hausa merchants in Maradi, the *Alhazai*, possess both material wealth and richness in men.

The honorific *Alhaji* originates in Islam—it is accorded to Muslims who have made the pilgrimage to Mecca.[2] The *Alhazai* are Muslims who respect the principles of Islam and its rules (fasting during Ramadan, abstinence from alcohol, prayer several times a day, etc.). They are not "sages," however, equal to the merchants of Senegal, nor is their knowledge of the Quran profound, even though many of them attended quranic schools.[3] In the Hausa country the title *Alhaji* has become a symbol of economic success: the pilgrimage to Mecca is the first major expense of any successful individual.[4] One can even say that the religious aspect, not to demean its importance, is less significant than the economic. This is not a recent development: Claude Meillassoux has noted that in the Sahara, trade brought with it Islam, the merchants participating actively in diffusing their religion.[5]

The accumulation of wealth by the *Alhazai* during the colonial and postcolonial periods heralded a new social hierarchy: if the city is a base for important merchants, it has also been the crucible for forming a class of small artisans, merchants, apprentices, and various other workers precariously living from day to day solely by the fruits of their own labor. What is going on in a city like Maradi is partly the formation of new social groups and partly the emergence of a new organization of social and economic relations. It is in such towns that the new Hausa society is being forged.

In the present work I propose to analyze the development of Maradi since its foundation but also to examine the city's social dynamics, in particular the appearance of a merchant bourgeoisie symbolized by the *Alhazai*, whose economic as well as other (e.g., ethnographic and religious) behaviors are well worth examination.

Given Maradi's many rural connections, an understanding of the countryside is clearly necessary before one can undertake an investigation of the urban setting. A number of studies done between 1976 and 1980 in the *département* of Maradi are especially helpful.[6]

Urban studies demand a multidisciplinary approach: the city is not the domain solely of geography or any other single discipline. On the contrary, one understands cities more easily thanks to differing insights. Thus, in addition to using the tools of geography (terrain studies, statistical analyses, etc.) I draw upon those of economics, history, and anthropology, fields whose methods are invaluable in tackling social phenomena. The study that follows lies at the crossroads of several disciplines.

The study is divided into an Introduction, which provides background to the study, and five chapters, and some general conclusions. Chapter 1 lays the groundwork for the research (the historic, geographic, and economic contexts) and reviews the principal characteristics of Maradi (population, location). Chapters 2 through 5 trace Maradi's political and economic history, distinguishing its three major stages: as a precolonial stronghold of prestigious and warlike chieftains (Chapter 2), major administrative and trading center (Chapter 3), and regional metropole (Chapter 4).

The tracing of the city's growth provides an opportunity to delineate the emergence of the *Alhazai*, who appear progressively during the colonial period but are even more prominent after Niger's independence.[7] From that time on, not only a business bourgeoisie settles into place but also a state and, as a consequence, a political and bureaucratic class whose relations with the merchant class at times have involved conflict, at times complicity. Finally, a teasing apart of the information thus accumulated reveals the social content of Maradi's development (Chapter 5), permitting some reflection upon the types of social relations that appear there. The general conclusions following Chapter 5 consider briefly some implications of these social changes.

NOTES

1. P. Chaunu and R. Gascon, *Histoire économique et sociale de la France*, Tome 1: *De 1450 à 1660*; Vol. 1: *l'Etat et la ville* (Paris: Presses Universitaires de France, 1977).
2. The Hausa variant is preferred here to the Arabic term (*El Hadj*).
3. Cf. Jean Copans, *Les marabouts de l'arachide* (Paris: Sycomore, 1980).
4. The role played by the title *Alhaji* in the world of commerce is perhaps similar to that of *sarkin noma* (master farmer) in the world of Hausa agriculture. This distinction is earned through completing the *dubu* ritual, during which the *sarkin noma* must collect and distribute a thousand sheaves of millet, as well as many gifts, to his followers so that they may benefit from his good fortune.
5. Claude Meillassoux, introduction to *The Development of Indigenous Trade and Markets in West Africa*, ed. International African Institute (Oxford: Oxford University Press, 1971).

6. E.g., the Campaign Against Tropical Aridity, the theme of whose research was "the study of disequilibria in natural, agricultural, and socioeconomic systems in the region of Maradi, Niger, with suggestions for a new agricultural development policy."

7. The precolonial period will be dealt with very briefly because the rise of the *Alhazai*, the central theme of this study, occurred after that period had ended.

1

Framework of the Study: The City and Its Environment

Without retracing all of West Africa's prehistory and antiquity, it is worthwhile to give some indication of its history and principal economic characteristics prior to the European penetration. This review will permit a better framing of the subject region and city in their African context.

HISTORY AND ECONOMY OF WEST AFRICA DURING THE PRECOLONIAL PERIOD

The review begins with what Jean Suret-Canale calls the "Middle Ages." According to Suret-Canale, "the term that situates a period between antiquity and modern times presupposes no specific duration, that duration clearly not being the same in black Africa and in Europe. In any case, as in Europe, in Africa the period running from the first centuries of the Christian era to the fifteenth and sixteenth centuries presents an incontrovertible unity."[1]

One of the characteristics of this period and the centuries immediately following was the appearance of the first large African states, politically organized and at times exercising very extensive economic influence on the continent.

The First Large States

Historians record the kingdom of Ghana among the earliest West African states; economic exchanges between the Sudan and North Africa, by way of the western Sahara, began during its formative stages. As early as the eighth century (Christian era) the Arab writers mention Ghana as a "country of

5

gold," to which North African merchants traveled in order to exchange their products with blacks from the gold-producing regions.

Ghana's hegemony declined from the eleventh century on and was later (in the thirteenth century) replaced by that of the empire of Mali, which was created under the leadership of one of its principal *sarkis*, Soundiata, who is still celebrated in oral legend.

The empire of Mali appears to have reached its zenith in the fourteenth century: at the empire's maximum extension, its authority ran from the kingdom of Songhai at Gao in the east all the way to the Atlantic coast in the west. As with Ghana, Mali's strength lay in trading gold for goods across the Sahara. This commercial expansion permitted the rise of two major cities, Timbuktu and Djenné; the first, created by the Tuareg in the thirteenth century, became a very dynamic market center whose activity gradually supplanted that of Oualata, an earlier, large Saharan city. Parallel to its commercial role, Timbuktu was also a religious center, whose population grew rapidly during the fifteenth century, reaching at least 25,000 inhabitants. As for Djenné, it had 10,000 to 15,000 inhabitants by the sixteenth century, playing the role of "port" city to trans-Saharan caravans, concentrating the products of Sudanese origin and redistributing merchandise imported from North Africa.[2]

In the fourteenth century the empire of Mali began to decay, its power weakened by quarrels within the royal family. The decay continued as attacks against Mali multiplied during the following century. The attacks were mounted by formerly submissive states that had freed themselves from the empire's authority. Its principal adversary was the kingdom of Songhai, which emancipated itself at the end of the fourteenth century and became the empire of Gao during the next (Map 1.1).

After annexing Timbuktu and Djenné and considerably weakening Mali, the empire of Songhai seized numerous other territories. At its height, Songhai reached from the lower Senegal River to the mountains of the Aïr range and the borders of Bornou in the east. Its authority thus extended over regions belonging to the modern Republic of Niger, such as Agadez, large areas along both banks of the Niger River, and a part of the Hausa country. Economically, Songhai's role was not inconsiderable: it developed trans-Saharan trade, attracting traders from Tripoli to Timbuktu and to its capital at Gao, and it remained influential until the end of the sixteenth century.

Further to the east, on the banks of Lake Chad, the same period saw the rise of the empire of Bornou, successor to the empire of Kanem, which had originated in the ninth century. At the end of the thirteenth century, Kanem stretched from Bilma and Tibesti in the north to Bornou in the west, and it had conquered the Fezzan, thus increasing the strategic importance of the oases of Kaouar and Djado. Relations with the Mediterranean probably account for the Fezzan's economic and political development, just as in the case of the western Sudan.

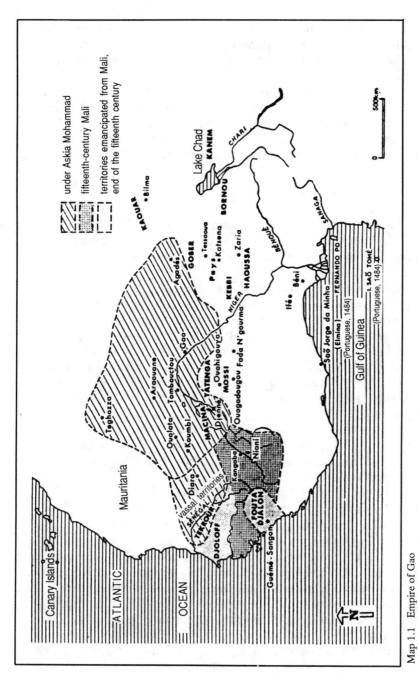

Map 1.1 Empire of Gao
Source: Suret-Canale, *Afrique noire; géographie—civilisation—histoire*

Destroyed during the fourteenth century, the empire of Kanem was reconstituted under the name of Bornou during the following century. Bornou expanded over a large area during the sixteenth century and extended its influence as far west as Damagaram.

During the sixteenth century, the territory lying within modern Niger was divided, the west being controlled by the empire of Songhai and the east by the empire of Bornou. Nevertheless, between these two great empires, the Hausa states gradually became established. Today, with the exception of Gobir, they lie mostly within the Republic of Nigeria.

The Hausa States

According to oral tradition, around the tenth century the Hausa people were created by the fusion of immigrants from the north and east—from Aïr and Bornou—with the local sedentary populations, giving rise to seven Hausa nations (*Hausa Bakwai*).[3]

The Hausa were not conquerors; they suffered repeated encroachments and suzerainties by neighboring empires (Songhai in the west, Bornou in the east). However, they gradually freed themselves from servitude, achieving a remarkable economic development during the seventeenth and eighteenth centuries. The commercial routes they opened during the fifteenth century between the central Sudan and the countries to the south (Gonja, Ashanti, and along the Gulf of Guinea) generated so much activity that a portion of the trans-Saharan trade shifted toward their towns after the fall of the empire of Songhai in 1591. In addition, their capitals (Kano, Katsina, Zaria, etc.) established permanent contact with the Mediterranean ports of Algiers and Tripoli (in Libya), becoming major commercial centers encompassing tens of thousands of inhabitants (at Kano, for example) and influencing trade in distant places.

At the beginning of the nineteenth century, having built prosperous cities and strong political structures, the Hausa found themselves confronted by a rebellion of the Peuls.[4] A young Peul marabout, Usman dan Fodio, who had been counselor to the sultan of Gobir, Baoua Jan Gorzo (reigned 1776–1784), decided to purify the local of version of Islam, which contained pagan beliefs and practices, and to put an end to burdensome taxes levied against the poor. He mounted a *jihad* (holy war) against the Hausa and Bornou dynasties and undertook to seize all the territories between the Niger River and Lake Chad. His Peul troops successively conquered several cities, including Kano, Katsina, and Zaria, and destroyed others, such as Birnin-Konni and Alkalawa (the latter was the capital of Gobir, which had been the first state to take up arms against Usman dan Fodio). The history of Maradi and its region was marked by these events. Throughout the nineteenth century Maradi was the seat of ousted Hausa princes and their descendants, who sought to reclaim their fiefs from the Peuls.

The arrival of the Europeans and the colonial conquest at the end of the century fixed these belligerents in their existing positions and pacified the region. In so doing, colonialism helped create new political systems.

THE BIRTH OF A NEW ENTITY: NIGER

The European occupation that started in the final years of the nineteenth century had been preceded by several decades of explorations, among them the expedition of Heinrich Barth, who, departing from Tripoli, traversed the entire central valley of the Niger before going on to Chad.[5]

From the time of its earliest missions, the French military's principal concern was to conclude treaties of alliance and protection with local authorities—for example, in the Djerma territories with the sultans of Kebi, in central Niger with the sultan of Tessaoua, and in the east with the *sarki* of the N'Guigmi. These missions had to do with protecting the population but also with surveying the terrain in expectation of further penetration and in hope of inhibiting exploration by other European nations.[6]

The central Sudan was conquered in stages, the initial French penetration being carried out in two operational phases: beginning from Dori (Burkina Faso), the conquest of the country up to and including the Niger River; then the linkage between Niger and Chad, at first badly carried out by the Voulet-Chanoine mission but then completed by the Joalland-Meynier mission. From 1899 on, a network of French outposts covered the new territory.

The passage from traditional political organization to colonial domination followed swiftly upon completion of the first treaties. The decree of November 20, 1900, created a new geographic division, the Third Military Territory, encompassing the regions between the Niger River and Lake Chad and delimited in the south by British possessions. This Third Military Territory, whose headquarters were at Zinder, was the administrative unit until January 1, 1911, when a civilian government was established at Zinder.

The decree of November 4, 1920, reorganized the area, which took the name Territory of Niger (January 1, 1921), soon transformed into the Colony of Niger (decree of October 13, 1922) with administrative and financial autonomy, placed under the direction of a lieutenant governor and the higher authority of the governor general of West Africa, resident at Dakar. Later, the administrative seat was transferred permanently from Zinder to Niamey (decree of December 28, 1926).

French authority over these new territories was not really complete until the beginning of the 1930s. Pacification was not achieved without resistance, at times fierce, from local peoples: a Djerma revolt (1906), an abortive attempt to assassinate the Europeans at Zinder (1906), and above all the general uprising of the Tuareg in 1916–1917, led by Sarki Kaossen in the Aïr Mountains.

Military and administrative domination was followed by economic exploitation. In Niger, as in other French colonies, this manifested itself through establishment of a trading economy based upon exportation of groundnuts (peanuts) and the distribution of imports, thus opening new outlets for the industries of the metropole.

The flowering of this trade economy did not reach substantial dimensions in Niger until after World War II, some time after it occurred in Senegal and Nigeria. As a result, the period 1939–1945 was one of isolation and uncertainty, although the colony did participate in the war effort. Economic recovery did not begin until 1946. From then on, groundnut commercialization recovered and began to generate steadily increasing tonnages.

An evolution of colonial policy also began in 1946, the French constitution of October 27, 1946, having transformed the former colonies into overseas territories integrated into the French union. Niger received a seat in the French National Assembly, a seat soon occupied by Diori Hamani.

The creation of several political parties enlivened Niger's politics: the Parti Progressiste Nigerien (PPN), which adhered in 1947 to the Rassemblement Democratique Africain (RDA, founded in Côte d'Ivoire) and counted among its ranks the territory's first deputy, Diori Hamani; the Union des Nigériens Indépendants et Sympathisants (UNIS, created by the French administration for its local sympathizers).[7] These were followed by the Union Progressiste Nigérienne (UPN), a 1953 offshoot of UNIS; the Union Démocratique Nigérienne (UDN), a 1954 offshoot of the RDA, led by Djibo Bakari; and the Bloc Nigérien d'Action (BNA), founded after a renewed schism within UNIS. In 1956 the BNA and the UDN joined to form the Mouvement Socialiste Africain (MSA), whose slogan, *sawaba* (freedom), eventually became the party's name.

The framework law of June 23, 1956, totally restructured Niger's political physiognomy by instituting a Council of Government whose chair was the governor but whose vice-president was elected by the Territorial Assembly and whose members were ministers. Parliamentary maneuvering brought Djibo Bakari to the vice-presidency and awarded the council memberships to a team of ministers representing the Sawaba Party. Nevertheless, the new constitution, proposed for referendum by France and approved by Niger, changed the political system yet again. A new Territorial Assembly was elected and began deliberations, and on December 18, 1958, it adopted a statute making Niger a republic and a member of the French community of nations. A new constitution was adopted on March 12, 1959, and, following the ineluctable evolution of other French African territories, Niger proclaimed its independence on August 3, 1960. Diori Hamani was elected by the assembly as president of the republic.

THE INDEPENDENT STATE

Diori Hamani was reelected president of the republic at the expiration of his first term and then a second time in 1970. Similarly, there were national assembly elections; only members of the PPN/RDA Party, which had become the sole legal party, were elected to the assembly.[8]

On April 15, 1974, President Hamani was overthrown by senior Nigerien military officers under the leadership of Lieutenant Colonel (later General) Seyni Kountché, who formed a Supreme Military Council that suspended the constitution of 1960, dissolved the National Assembly, and suppressed all political activity.[9] Kountché attached a high priority to restoring efficiency to the government's administration, which he accused of negligence and corruption, and to relaunching the country's economy, at that time very much disrupted by a severe drought.

Accession to independence, despite the changes it set in motion in the organization of commerce (disappearance of the European commercial houses from the trade economy and creation of state-owned firms to replace them), did not change the Nigerien economy profoundly: groundnuts and livestock remained the country's principal export products. Groundnut production increased in the course of the 1960s, reaching its apogee during the 1966–1967 harvest, when 191,307 metric tons were collected. The rainfall deficits registered at the beginning of the 1970s reversed this trend, and the drought dealt it a fatal blow. Commercialization eventually reached very low levels (1,400 metric tons in 1983–1984). Rural communities having abandoned groundnuts in favor of foodstuffs as a cash crop following the drought, Niger lost its principal source of monetary wealth.

The exploitation of uranium deposits, discovered by the French Commissariat à l'Energie Atomique (CEA) along the southern and eastern edges of the Aïr Mountains, became the substitute for the cultivation of groundnuts, furnishing essential financial resources to the government of Niger (Figure 1.1). Steady increases in production, coupled with rising prices for uranium (a kilogram of which sold for 10,000 CFA francs in 1975 and 24,000 in 1979) yielded the country substantial budgetary receipts (Table 1.1).

This improvement in the country's financial situation permitted the government to take a number of steps (suspension of taxes and creation of development projects) to help rural communities severely injured by the drought and to implement investment programs (construction of roads, dispensaries, schools, etc.) intended to modernize the countryside. These programs were defined in the five-year plan for 1979–1983, which gave priority to regional development—a judicious choice, given the country's huge size and contrasting territories.

From 1982 on, the economic situation deteriorated as a result of falling

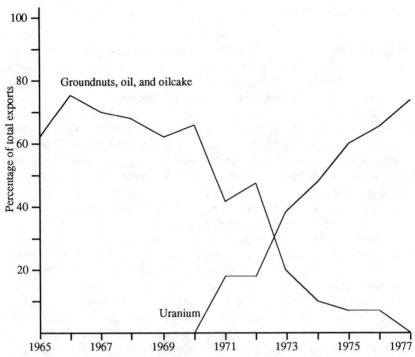

Figure 1.1   Comparative Changes in Groundnut and Uranium Exports as a
            Percentage of Total Exports
Source: Republic of Niger, *Annuaire statistique 1978–1979*

Table 1.1   Niger's National Budget (in billions of CFA francs)

Year	Budget
1970	10.8
1974	14.2
1975	15.3
1976	24.3
1977	34.1
1978	43.4
1979	56.7
1980	72.1
1981	80.6
1982	93.8
1983	81.2
1984	80.2

Source: Ministry of Finance, Niamey

world prices for uranium (to 20,000 CFA francs per kilogram in 1981), throwing the balance of trade into a major deficit. General Seyni Kountché referred to this in a speech delivered on April 15, 1983: "The crisis whose perniciousness we fearfully anticipated has now come to pass in our country. Every family feels its effects; every Nigerien must endure it."

To combat the economic crisis that threatened the national budget, the government took steps to improve public management (by slashing government expenditures and reducing personnel) and to put the brakes on imports. These measures were accompanied by a liberalization of the economy to the advantage of the private sector, a process encouraged by the IMF and the World Bank, not only in Niger but also in other African countries.

THE REGION AROUND MARADI

Following independence in 1960, the government of Niger undertook to legislate the many measures necessary to the proper functioning of a nation-state; among them, it provided (in 1964) an administrative reorganization into seven *départements*, themselves subdivided into *arrondissements* (Map 1.2).

The *département* of Maradi is situated in south-central Niger, delimited to the east by the *département* of Zinder, to the west by that of Tahoua, and to the north by that of Agadez. In the south, it has a common frontier, established during the colonial era, with the Federal Republic of Nigeria. Within its boundaries the *département* covers 38,500 square kilometers, or 3 percent of Niger's total area (Map 1.3).

The national census conducted in December 1977 counted 944,288 inhabitants for the *département*, or an average density of twenty-four persons per square kilometer, making it the most densely populated *département* in Niger.[10] This population, whose growth is very rapid (the annual rate was 3.1 percent between 1960 and 1977), is extremely young: about 45 percent of the inhabitants are less than fifteen years old. Finally, it is largely rural (90.4 percent in 1977), having only two towns—Maradi and Tessaoua—exceeding 10,000 inhabitants (Map 1.4).

Aside from the Hausa, who make up the majority in the area under study, other ethnic groups include the Peul, the Beri-beri (originally from the kingdom of Bornou, they have been progressively assimilated to the Hausa, adopting their language and a number of their customs), the Bouzou (former captives of the Tuareg), and the Tuareg (who are settling more and more in the pastoral zone and in areas bordering the *départements* of Tahoua and Agadez). The spatial distribution of the different groups depends upon their activity (farming or herding), the agricultural zone in the south of the

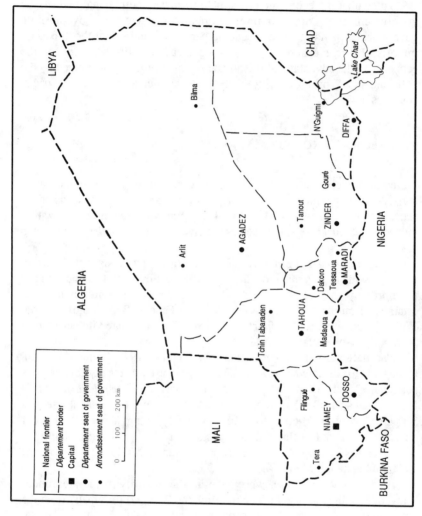

Map 1.2   A New Entity: The Republic of Niger

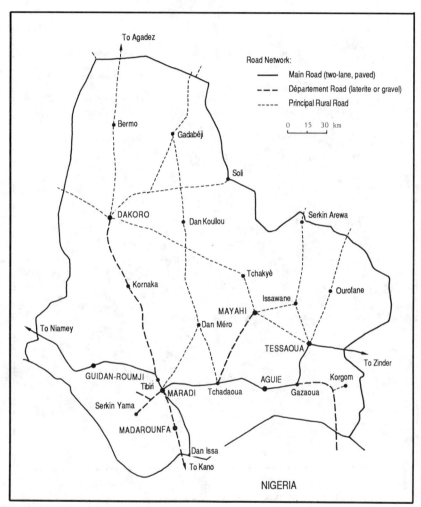

Map 1.3 *Département* of Maradi

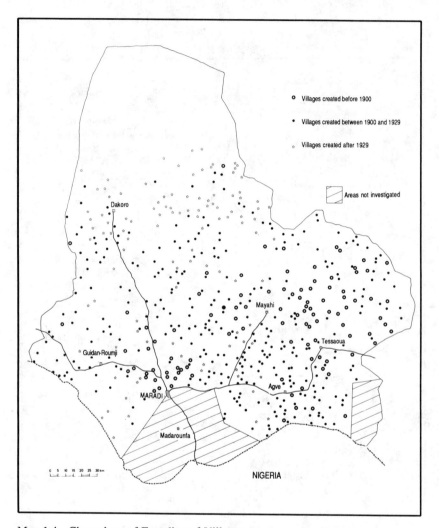

Map 1.4   Chronology of Founding of Villages
Source: Grégoire and Raynaut, "Présentation générale du département de Maradi"

département being more populated than the pastoral zone along the Dakoro–Sarkin Arewa axis. This strong preponderance of rural population confirms that farming and herding play an important role, providing essential resources to the *département*'s inhabitants.

Recent research results provide evidence of major problems confronting agricultural and pastoral production efforts.[11] The drought set in motion profound modifications in the production and commercialization of agricultural products: the key factor is the net drop in groundnut culture (the Maradi region was the "groundnut basket" of Niger) in favor of food-grain production (millet and sorghum), a change whose effects were painfully severe. As for livestock production, it too suffered grave effects, and herders were among those hit hardest during the years of scarcity that decimated their herds.

In recent years, the situation appears to have improved steadily: the herds have now been almost completely reconstituted and food sufficiency is achieved whenever rainfall is satisfactory. There remain a few problems that could lead to disastrous consequences in the event of another drought:

- The precariousness of food production among the peasants,
- Weakness of farm revenues and small size of productive investments,
- Competition between agricultural and pastoral activities involving communities of farmers versus communities of herders, and
- The exodus from the countryside into the towns.[12]

The last point is a recent phenomenon, and the drought appears to have had much to do with accelerating it. The exodus is a true mass movement, affecting all parts of the region studied.[13] One would imagine it is due to diverse and general causes at the basic level of economic and social organization. We need to examine the relationship between the functioning of agropastoral production systems and the difficulties such systems encounter.

This exodus is most often temporary—a few months, generally divided into several repeated stays—and affects mainly young males (under thirty years of age). It is oriented primarily toward cities in Nigeria: Kano, Katsina, Kaduna, Bauchi, and even Lagos. A small proportion of the migrants remain in Niger; some go to work in the uranium mines at Arlit, whereas others head for centers such as Niamey, Zinder, or Maradi.

THE CITY OF MARADI

The analysis above is intended to provide a regional context, a background for understanding the city; it remains to examine Maradi itself.[14]

Population

The principal difficulty in studying an African population lies in the credibility one can assign to numerical data. Figures for Maradi are few and uncertain prior to 1950, the year in which the census began to be conducted regularly. Nevertheless, it is possible to distinguish two phases in Maradi's demographic evolution:[15] the first involves moderate growth over four decades (1909–1950); the second is marked by a demographic upsurge covering the past three decades.

The Period 1909–1950

Maradi experienced a very weak average rate of annual growth (1.7 percent) and its population did not even double during the period, since it rose only from 4,500 inhabitants (1911) to about 8,700 in 1950. The limits to growth had several causes: During the nineteenth century, the spatial location of villages was discontinuous, for reasons of security. The region was a refuge for Hausa populations that opposed the Peuls. Colonization put an end to ethnic confrontations and set in motion a wave of expansion into empty spaces: the installation in the bush of residents from heavily populated areas—Maradi and the valley of the Maradi River (*Goulbin* Maradi)—was rendered possible by the security farmers were now able to enjoy (see Map 1.4). This positive aspect of the French presence had, however, its negative counterpart: the colonial government's measures taken in times of peace (requisitions, forced labor, various taxes) impelled townspeople to migrate into the bush or even to Nigeria. Epidemics and famines, often deadly, also contributed to the stagnation of population growth in Maradi and stimulated emigration into Nigeria. Finally, after the 1945 flood in Maradi (which actually killed very few people), some residents (again very few, no doubt) refused to move to the newly built section of town and instead moved into the bush.

These diverse elements explain the weak demographic growth during the period under examination. The phenomenon occurred in other towns of Niger, whose growth also stagnated even though that of the territory grew from 890,000 inhabitants in 1913 to 1.75 million in 1936.[16]

In 1950 Maradi was the fourth largest urban area in Niger, exceeded by Niamey (11,790), Tahoua (10,748), and Zinder (9,500 inhabitants). Its population had begun to grow in 1945 with the ending of forced labor and the *indigénat*, and then more and more rapidly a bit later as the groundnut trade mushroomed (Table 1.2).[17]

The Period 1950–1983

The 1950s marked a demographic revival, with Maradi growing from 8,660 inhabitants in 1950 to 12,500 in 1959. This rate of growth increased further during the 1960s, the high point of the groundnut trade. While generating additional employment within itself, the groundnut trade also had multiple repercussions on other economic activities (transport, construction, oil processing, etc.), making the city more and more attractive to laborers from the surrounding countryside. This impact is illustrated in Table 1.3.

From 1970 on, the difficulties encountered by the peasants during and after the drought accelerated the rural exodus that now affects all Sahelian countries. It has caused cities such as Maradi to double their populations in the space of ten years (from 28,000 inhabitants in 1970 to 66,472 in 1981).

In the context of weak Nigerien urban growth rates (11.8 percent in 1977), Niamey (12 percent), Maradi (8.25 percent), and Agadez (8 percent) have the highest rates of demographic growth (8.25 percent). This dynamism is due to the natural growth rate (about 3.9 percent per year) plus the rural exodus (about 4.4 percent per year), still strong but normal for an African city of moderate importance.[18]

Table 1.2   Population Growth in Maradi

Year	Population
1911	4,502
1921	6,539
1930	7,017
1931	6,700
1936	7,358
1944	8,353
1950	8,661
1959	12,500
1970	28,784
1977	45,852
1981	66,472
1983	80,000

Table 1.3   Population of Maradi: Average Annual Rate of Growth

Period	Percentage
1950–1959	4.25
1959–1970	7.85
1970–1980	8.25
1950–1980	6.85

The Urban Space

The old city was situated in the valley along the banks of the Maradi River, an intermittent waterway whose source lies in Nigeria. The palace of the provincial *sarki* and the homes of notables doubtless dominated the majority of huts. The town, roughly circular in form, was protected by a wall of *banco* (mud brick) pierced by four gates (Map 1.5). This configuration was altered by the colonial government, which installed its infrastructures (residence, guardhouse, etc.) on the plateau overlooking the town. Also, in 1912 the government built a main road cutting the old town into two parts and linking the guardhouse with the commercial quarter and the central market (Map 1.6).

At the end of the rainy season of 1945, the Maradi River attained an exceptional water level and inundated the town entirely except for the groundnut oil mill and a few multistory commercial buildings. In order to prevent a recurrence of the catastrophe, the authorities moved the entire town up onto the plateau (December 1945), completely changing Maradi's appearance. Its new, checkerboard design was bounded by orthogonal axes and focused upon a vast circular space around which were built the palace of the provincial *sarki* and the main mosque. The commercial district was relocated to the town's east side and the market was placed in the new town center, while the administrative quarter remained at its initial location because it was already on the plateau and thus had not suffered at all from the flooding. This section, made up of various town offices, is unmistakably stamped by its typical colonial architecture (Map 1.7).[19]

Maradi's geographic growth was relatively slow until the 1950s, when it accelerated along with the development of the groundnut trade. Next to older neighborhoods, new ones grew up, such as Sabon Gari (settled in 1957) and Sabon Carré (1963).

Urban growth speeded up in the course of the 1970s, notably after the arrival of numerous rural migrants at the time of the drought. In addition, during this period Maradi acted as a magnet in the region, its administrative functions having been expanded (Maradi being the seat of the national government's departmental services for the area) and its industrial sector strengthened by the installation of several factories.

The geographic expansion stimulated the settlement of several other neighborhoods (Soura Bouldé in 1977, Tarna in 1978, and Zaria in 1981) and led to the elaboration in 1973 of a general city plan, later revised. It is worth noting that the policies pursued were coherent and allowed the authorities to avoid being overwhelmed by demographic growth—the town produced no large slums. Prospects for development are encouraging because Maradi has large, well-placed land reserves, notably along the road leading toward Niamey. The town might also link up with Tibiri, traditional capital of the Hausa territory of Gobir, some 7 kilometers distant (Map 1.8).

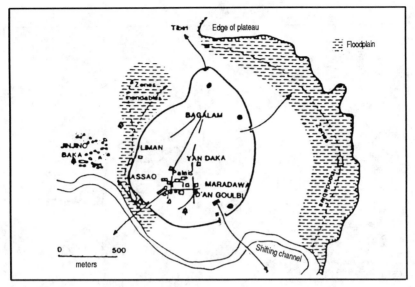

Map 1.5   Maradi Prior to Colonial Rule

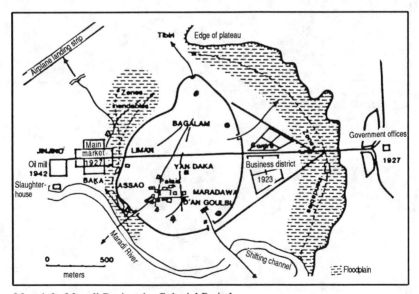

Map 1.6   Maradi During the Colonial Period

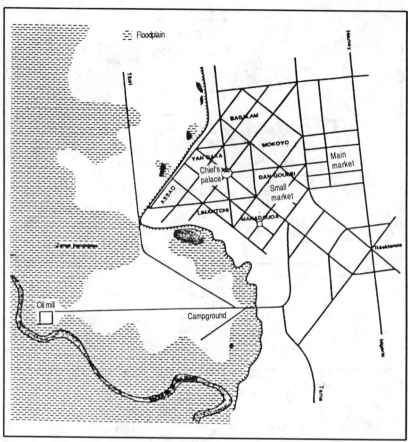

Map 1.7   Maradi After the Reconstruction of 1945
Source: David, "Maradi, l'ancien Etat et l'ancienne ville"

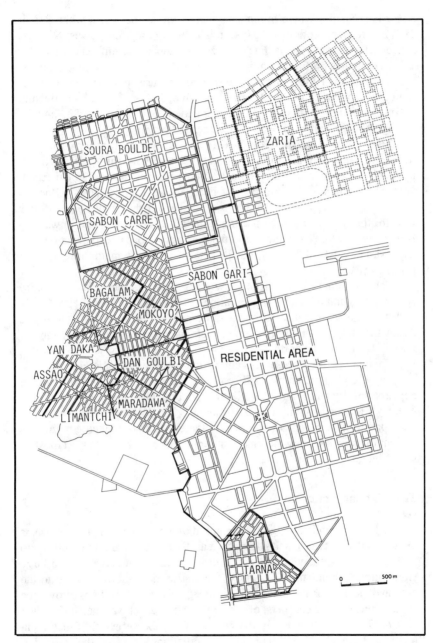

Map 1.8   Modern Maradi

Maradi in the Urban Context of Niger

Niger is a country where minimal urbanization has occurred, where (as of 1977) there were more than 30,000 inhabitants in only four towns: Niamey, Zinder, Maradi, and Tahoua. Each of these developed on a different basis.

Niamey has profited from its political and administrative functions and has become, over the years, a true capital because it is the center of the region's economic, political, administrative, industrial, and intellectual activities.[20] Its population was estimated at 350,000 in 1983, and its demographic growth remains strong (12 percent per year).

Zinder was a prosperous place in the nineteenth century, thanks to trans-Saharan trade. Its influence declined after the Europeans arrived, although they made it the colonial capital of Niger until 1926. In recent years, its economic growth has not been as rapid as Maradi's, although Zinder appears now to be getting a second wind that may generate new growth: the improvement of the road linking it to Agadez and onward to Algiers may restore its former importance as a crossroads. Its population now approximates that of Maradi, but its rate of growth remains inferior (6.5 percent a year).

Tahoua remains a market town for contacts between sedentary communities and nomads. Its population (31,000 in 1977) fluctuates widely with the seasons because a considerable number of the inhabitants leave during the rainy season for the farm hamlets spread across the countryside and for the pastures in the north.

Compared with these other centers and given its considerable assets—proximity to Nigeria, ample land reserves, and sizable population—Maradi appears solidly ensconced as Niger's second city, a counterweight to Niamey's preponderant influence. If Maradi's initial development was due in good part to its location at the center of the groundnut-producing region, its current dynamism is now due more and more to the links it has established with Nigeria.

The Nigerian Connection

The Federal Republic of Nigeria, composed of nineteen states (as of 1982), is the leading country of black Africa by reason of its population (85 million to 100 million), its economic power, and its political influence. Three large ethnic groups dominate the country: the Hausa in the north, the Ibo in the east, and the Yoruba in the west. Their antagonisms have at times thrown the country into bloody conflicts, of which the most recent was the Biafran war (1967–1970), which ended in the failure of the Ibo secession. Since then, there has been an effort at national reconciliation. President Shehu Shagari was chosen by national elections in 1979 and reelected in 1983. The second mandate lasted only a short time, as Shagari was overthrown on December 31, 1983, by General Mohammed Buhari, who was in turn deposed (August 1985) by General Ibrahim Babangida.

Thanks to a considerable increase in the production and the price of oil, the country's principal export resource, Nigeria benefited from very substantial revenues, which the government used to launch a series of development programs in every sector of the economy. In addition to industrialization, the transfer of the seat of the federal government to Abuja (a site at the center of the country) is one of the most prestigious of the projects, intended to reduce the overpopulation of the present capital, Lagos.

Since 1981 Nigeria has encountered serious difficulties resulting from a fall in oil production and oil prices brought on by a glut in global markets. This has obliged the government to take painful countermeasures, limiting expenses and attempting to protect the domestic economy.[21]

Within Nigeria, the north has long seemed a coherent and monolithic bloc, organized around the Hausa language and around the dominant religion, Islam, which still has vigorously active adherents (as demonstrated by insurrections in Kano, Maiduguri, and Kaduna during the early 1980s). Today the Hausa hold a decisive position in the emerging nation-state, controlling essential levers of power.[22] Their enterprising spirit, as Guy Nicolas notes, is the wind that has driven the Hausa merchants to monopolize a large part of commerce in southern Nigeria.

The euphoria accompanying the petroleum boom provoked a major rural exodus and uncontrolled urbanization, especially in the north: cities such as Kano (more than 1.5 million inhabitants), Kaduna, Zaria, Bauchi, Sokoto, Katsina, Gusau, and Maiduguri attracted tens of thousands of immigrants. Some of these are ancient towns whose prosperity once depended upon trans-Saharan trade.

Because of its history and its common civilization with northern Nigeria, Maradi maintains close ties with that country. These relations are not solely social but also economic, including commercial: there is a very active and often illegal trade all along the frontier. These activities were especially significant during the Biafran war, which cut off the north from its normal links to the sea. Maradi thus played an important role in provisioning its neighbors, and a great variety of merchandise, imported via Cotonou or Lomé, was introduced into northern Nigeria from Maradi.

Although now somewhat diminished, these exchanges have continued despite the closing of the frontier. The local merchants, the *Alhazai*, use Maradi as a transit point for goods whose import into Nigeria is theoretically prohibited, the measures having been taken in order to protect Nigeria's national industries. This commercial activity in large part explains the current dynamism of Maradi.

CONCLUSION

A major break in the history of West Africa occurred within the past century as a result of colonization: the Europeans established new social groupings, an unintended effect of their military conquests. They created artificial frontiers that cut across previously homogeneous regions and separated peoples formerly united. The case of Maradi, brutally cut off from northern Nigeria, of which it had once been a part, illustrates clearly the arbitrary character of the colonial demarcations. The political domination was followed by similarly imperialistic economic measures that exploited local resources for the profit of distant metropoles or introduced new activities (groundnut cultivation in the Sahel, for example) for production of exports.

A second major historical rupture occurred with the accession of these territories to independence and the establishment of numerous sovereign states. If this change was necessary politically, it was less so economically for several countries, which continued to put their resources into activities introduced under colonialism (such as groundnut culture in Niger and Senegal).

The economic transformation took place later, during the 1970s. A global economic crisis affected the African countries, which encountered grave financial problems, in particular growing foreign debt due to deterioration in their terms of trade. Also, as their dependence upon international agencies (the IMF, the World Bank, etc.) grew, they found their development strategies increasingly dictated from abroad.

While the majority of African countries experienced these problems, the Sahelian countries also had to face a long drought that undermined their efforts in agriculture and livestock raising, accentuating their other difficulties. In Niger, however, one can consider the 1970s a turning point: beyond the events of the world economic crisis and the drought, the country's economy was profoundly affected by exploitation of the uranium deposits in the Aïr Mountains, and to a lesser extent by the change of political regime in April 1974.

These comments on the general situation in West Africa, and more precisely on the situation in Niger, will be explored further at the regional and urban levels by examining the political and economic history of one city, Maradi. This is an ordinary city whose growth has been extremely rapid during the past twenty-five years, during which time its commercial character has also been transformed. Maradi's economic dynamism runs counter to the stagnation in the region's agricultural production, drawing instead upon the emergence of a merchant class, the *Alhazai*, whose political and economic influence has become important throughout Niger.

NOTES

1. J. Suret-Canale, *Afrique noire occidentale et centrale* (Paris: Editions Sociales, 1966).

2. Ibid.

3. The seven Hausa states are the following: Kano, Katsina, Zakzak (Zaria), Gobir, Rano, Ouangara, Daura.

4. This rebellion had already begun in other parts of West Africa before the end of the eighteenth century. [Peul is the French colloquial designation of the tribe known also as Fula or Fulbé, and in English as the Fulani—Translator.]

5. H. Barth, *Voyages et découvertes dans l'Afrique septentrionale et centrale pendant les années 1849 à 1855*, trans. P. Ithier (Paris: A. Bohné, 1860–1861), Vol. 3.

6. E. Sere de Rivières, *Histoire du Niger* (Paris: Berger-Levrault, 1965).

7. Ibid.

8. The other parties had been forced out of the Nigerien political system by the PPN/RDA.

9. Following a long illness, President Seyni Kountché died in Paris in November 1987. He was replaced as president of the republic (and of the Supreme Military Council) by Colonel Ali Saibou—Translator.

10. The valley of the Maradi River is the most densely populated zone in the region. It is also there that the earliest human settlements were located.

11. C. Raynaut, *Recherches multi-disciplinaires sur la région de Maradi: rapport de synthèse* (Bordeaux: University of Bordeaux II, 1980).

12. At the time the present study was first published, Niger found itself in such a delicate situation: during the rainy season of 1984, rainfall was far below normal, which would have threatened the population with famine had international food aid not been made available.

13. According to an inquiry covering 600 villages (the *département* contains about 2,150), 89 percent were affected by the exodus. Cf. E. Grégoire and C. Raynaut, *Présentation générale du département de Maradi* (Bordeaux: University of Bordeaux II, 1980).

14. For details, see E. Grégoire, "Développement urbain et accumulation marchande: les *Alhazai* de Maradi (Niger)," doctoral thesis, third cycle, University of Bordeaux III, 1983.

15. The absence of data makes demographic study of the precolonial period impossible.

16. G. Spittler, "Migrations rurales et développement économique: exemple du canton de Tibiri," unpublished, 1970.

17. The *indigénat* was an onerous French colonial legal system—Translator.

18. According to a recent study by Claude Herry, the rates of birth and mortality at Maradi are 5.9 percent and 1.85 percent, respectively. In absolute terms, Maradi's drain on its surrounding countryside remains weak (about 3,200 persons per year) and is probably less than that of Nigeria.

19. Maradi is a "horizontal" city, whose average population density is not great (113 inhabitants per hectare in 1980).

20. Sidikou Harouna Hamidou, "Niamey, étude de géographie socio-urbaine," doctoral thesis, University of Haute-Normandie (Rouen), 1980.

21. The decision taken in January 1983 to expel all foreigners whose documents where not in proper order appears to have been motivated by the

economic difficulties and the unemployment resulting therefrom. Similarly, the devaluation of May 1984 and the closing of land frontiers were intended to protect Nigeria's economy.

22. Guy Nicolas, "Le Nord est destiné à jouer un rôle majeur," *Le Monde,* October 18, 1981.

2

The Precolonial Site: Politics and Economics of Maradi in the Nineteenth Century

The history of Maradi and its region is closely related to that of the Hausa states, particularly Katsina. The legends surrounding the creation of Katsina (eleventh century A.D.) vary considerably among narrators. The relevant events surrounding the birth of the hamlet that became Maradi occur at a much more recent time, the end of the eighteenth century.

The founding of Maradi itself took place even later (1815), at a time of change, during which the Peul empire of Sokoto was growing at the expense of the Hausa states. The birth and development of Maradi, in the center of a region containing few people, is directly related to this event and to the desire of the princes of the former Hausa states to regain their fiefs. The struggles that pitted the new state of Maradi against the emirate of Sokoto continued throughout the nineteenth century, not ending until the arrival of the Europeans, which fixed the belligerents in their existing positions (Map 2.1). Throughout the precolonial period, these events far overshadowed any economic activities occurring in Maradi.

MARADI'S EARLY HISTORY AND POLITICS

A precise and detailed chronology of Maradi's history has been provided elsewhere.[1] A review of the city's principal characteristics during the nineteenth century can be covered in three statements:

- Maradi was a town of recent origin, unlike other Hausa centers.
- It was the seat of a powerful chiefdom, well organized and warlike.
- Its political life during the last quarter of the century exhibited an instability that did not end until the arrival of the Europeans.

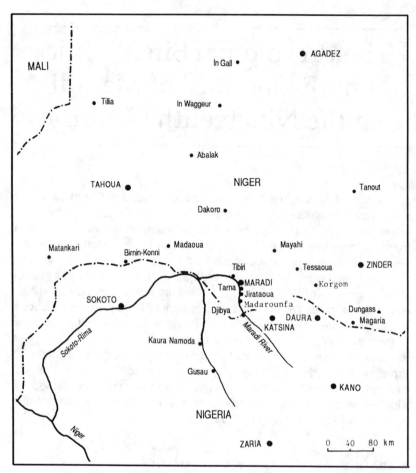

Map 2.1   Maradi and Its Region

A City of Recent Origin

The conflicts in which the state of Katsina opposed the state of Gobir eventually resulted at the end of the eighteenth century in victory for Katsina. The region of Maradi, formerly a theater of operations for the combatants, was settled by people of Katsina who came into the valley of the Maradi River in search of virgin farmland to replace lands abandoned further south. In small successive migratory waves, they established themselves in the valley and quickly assimilated the Anna, the autochthonous peoples who hunted and fished there.[2]

Probably during the eighteenth century, the *sarkis* of Katsina decided to exercise authority more directly over the population by appointing a representative. This measure was necessary because the people lived in a permanent state of insecurity, frequently under attack from slavers. The representative of Katsina was installed at first in the village of Riadi, but then moved his residence closer to Tarna, to a tiny farm hamlet where the present-day neighborhood called Maradaoua is located; the animists in the area occupied several buildings next to a white acacia tree, the *gawom* Barki. According to legend, one night a man called Barki, wanting a place to hang his quiver, drove a stick into the ground; in the course of the night, the stick grew to be a tree.[3] This man built several houses at the foot of the tree, thus becoming the founder of Maradi, although the name would come only later.[4]

The little community, living on a bit of farming, hunting, and gathering, was caught up in events at the beginning of the nineteenth century. This period, as already noted, was marked by the revolt of the Peuls, led by the marabout Usman dan Fodio, who mounted a *jihad* against the Hausa and Bornou dynasties and at their expense built a new empire—the empire of Sokoto.

Katsina, like the other Hausa cities, was captured and reorganized by the Peuls, who named a governor there, Malam Oumarou. No doubt moving into the region of Maradi from the south, Malam Oumarou confided its occupation to one of his lieutenants, Mani, who had no difficulty establishing his suzerainty.

According to witnesses, the Peuls were not content with systematic and profitable exploitation of the country; their domination was sometimes cruel.[5] Tilho writes: "The Peul horsemen terrorized the country, carrying their impudence to the point of demanding that husbands hold their horses' reins while they entered the compounds to violate the women."[6]

In the face of these effronteries and in order to escape the heavy tributes they were forced to pay, the Anna decided to revolt and requested the aid of Dan Kassawa, hereditary prince of the former state of Katsina who had taken refuge in Zinder. The prince demanded the head of Mani as an indication of the people's sincerity and desire to fight.

Organization of the rebellion against the Peuls was the work of a small band of Anna, mostly from the villages around the *gawom* Barki and from Soumarana. Details vary according to the recitation of the legend, but all versions agree that Mani was murdered, apparently decapitated at Soumarana. Dan Kassawa, seeing his condition fulfilled, arrived at Maradi with an army to take command of the rebellion begun by the Anna. His objective was to reconquer Katsina.

One of Dan Kassawa's first decisions was to move the various villages down into the valley of the Maradi River, where they would be less exposed to pillage and enemy assault than upon the plateau. A new village, Maradi, was therefore built into a tight clearing during 1815, the course of the river having been diverted.[7] Dan Kassawa had scarcely achieved this when the Peuls took up arms and attacked Maradi because the inhabitants had dared to rebel. There were many battles between the opposing armies, but the Peuls were never able to reconquer the area around Maradi. At his death (1830), Dan Kassawa had succeeded in ending direct military threats to any part of the state of Maradi.

These events, unfolding at the beginning of the nineteenth century, clearly show that Maradi is a town of recent origin, in contrast with Kano, Katsina, Zinder, and even Tessaoua, which are the ancient, historic towns. Nevertheless, even though relatively young, Maradi counts among its citizens representatives of the old Hausa culture, in the descendants of sovereigns of Katsina, Kano, and Gobir who came to take refuge. The people of Maradi are proud of their town, seat of a new state whose organization was modeled on that of the state of Katsina.

Political and Military Organization of the Chiefdom of Maradi During the Nineteenth Century

The reign of Dan Kassawa marked the installation of an independent power, gradually asserted: the new state was born despite having been considered temporary, the original objective having been the reconquest of Katsina. Gradually the inhabitants of Maradi, sensing themselves secure, undertook the colonization of the valley, founding several villages (Maradu, Gabi, etc.) along the banks of the Maradi River.

At his death, Dan Kassawa left his successors a solid entity, well organized according to old administrative traditions. At the summit was the Sarki/Katsina, who reigned over the entire territory and its subjects. Not designated by parental lineage, he was elected by a college (*rukuni*) composed of four of the state's highest officials. The powers of the *sarki* and of the electoral college were in equilibrium, and the state could not be governed well without their harmony.

The electoral college was subdivided into two groups clearly distinguishing military from civilian tasks: The left hand (*hannu na auni*) of the *sarki* (chief) included the war chief (the *kaura*), responsible for the army and for military operations, and also the chief of police (the *durbi*), a descendant of Katsina's founding dynasty, charged with maintaining respect for law and order within the country. The right hand (*hannu na dama*) of the *sarki* also comprised two officials: the *galadima* (usually a eunuch), charged with civil administration and the good order of the palace, and the *yan daka*, whose principal task was to assist the *galadima*.

The *kaura* and the *galadima* held the more important powers. In one way or another the four senior figures were assisted by a multitude of notables who together constituted the chiefdom (*sarauta*). During the reign of Dan Baskore (1851–1873) they totaled about 130, among whom there were several women.[8]

The judicial institutions of the state depended upon the *galadima*, who probably represented the *sarki*. Nevertheless, each member of the electoral college could exercise justice within a particular domain. The judicial system rested upon a collection of rules that were a synthesis of Islamic laws and animist practices.

State finances came from various sources: a tax imposed at harvest time represented one-tenth of the crop and was turned over to the village *sarkis*, who transmitted it to the *sarki*. The tax on commoners (*talakawa*) was levied each year in order to carry out various chores: repair of town walls, farm work in the chiefdom's fields, and so on. Other than these demands, there were taxes on merchants who traversed the region or who sold goods there. The various revenues assured the operation of the state apparatus and the maintenance of the chiefdom.

These institutions, put in place by Dan Kassawa, resembled structures that had once existed in Katsina, even though they also adapted certain practices of the indigenous animists into whose lands the Katsina refugees had fled. Dan Baskore strengthened them and extended Maradi's reach into the countryside.

Dan Baskore made Maradi a fortified and well-protected town, a veritable *birni*:[9] for the old enclosure of planks and pikes, he substituted a wall of pounded earth and stone, surrounded by a moat 4 meters wide and more than 2 meters deep. There were gates into the fortifications at the four corners, watched over by guards.

In addition to the organization of his state and its capital, Dan Baskore mounted several expeditions against the Peuls; he was the last *sarki* to attempt the recapture of Katsina. One of his offensives was repulsed only 6 kilometers from its objective; it involved nearly 6,000 men, mostly from Katsina but also contingents from Damagaram, Gobir, and Tuareg Kel Ewey.

A Time of Troubles:
From 1873 Until the Arrival of the Europeans

Dan Baskore died in 1873, and a glorious page in Maradi's history turned. The years following were marked by great political instability. The next *sarki* had neither Dan Baskore's authority nor his prestige; this created a pattern, each successor being overthrown after a few years, in some cases only a few months, in power. In 1890 the grandson of Dan Kassawa, Mijinyawa, was chosen Maradi's new leader. After a series of conflicts within the chiefdom, he took flight with most of his followers and found refuge at Tessaoua; there he founded a small independent principality, the sultanate of Tessaoua (1892).

At Maradi, this opened a period dominated by a man of forceful personality, Kaura Assao, who, after the flight of Mijinyawa, acceded to the official title of *kaura* despite his Peul origins (Maradi having previously awarded this position to Peuls who had offered their military skills). Kaura Assao became powerful enough to assert his will and to control the chiefdom's policies, even though he could not exercise it directly because others held nominal power. In this guise, according to Philippe David, he could even make and unmake Maradi's *sarkis*.[10]

The final decades of the nineteenth century were thus a period of political instability, of internal struggles involving various pretenders to the chiefdom, some of whom were manipulated by Kaura Assao. The period contrasted strongly with the earlier decades, when Maradi was strong and united. European penetration would profoundly alter the situation.

The first "whites" to reach Maradi were the men of Cazemajou's column (1898). They stayed only a few days, their objective being to reach Lake Chad, which they never attained, as they were captured and killed at Zinder by the sultan of Damagaram. They were followed a year later by Voulet-Chanoine's expedition to central Africa, still remembered painfully in Niger.[11]

Departing from the Sudan, the Voulet-Chanoine column intended to reach Lake Chad as quickly as possible in order to claim for France all the territory not yet occupied by the colonial powers.[12] Their progress eastward was bloody, involving massacres, pillage, and destruction of whole villages and towns (Matankari, Birnin-Konni, Tibiri). As the troops approached Maradi, their terrifying reputation preceding them, the *sarki* and his subjects sought refuge in the forest, where they hid for about two weeks. The French officers thus found an empty town, which they pillaged and burned before continuing toward the east. The tragic expedition ended at Tessaoua, where a column of regulars, led by Colonel Klobb, intercepted it and ended its misdeeds.[13] After the Voulet-Chanoine expedition, the French left the region alone for some years, although they divided it with the British, on paper at least, at conferences far away.

ECONOMIC LIFE IN THE REGION

In the parts of West Africa that border the desert, trade routes have had vital importance, the most heavily traveled being those across the Sahara. Secular commercial traffic crossed the Sahara, linking the Mediterranean ports (Algiers, Tunis, and especially Tripoli) to a number of towns in black Africa located between the Niger River and Lake Chad, the principal ones being Sokoto, Katsina, Kano, and Zinder.

The basis of caravan business, carried out by Tuareg and Arab camel drivers, was the trade in black slaves destined for the countries of the Maghreb, Egypt, and the Arabian Peninsula. It made the Hausa states of the eighteenth century into great commercial centers with large populations and control over vast regions. Katsina played the most important role in accumulating slaves, gold, ivory, cloth, and leather, which were exchanged for the products of North Africa: weapons, horses, fabrics, European and Turkish money, and other items.

The fratricidal struggles loosed by the many pretenders to the chiefdoms of Katsina and Gobir at the end of the eighteenth century affected Katsina's prosperity and weakened its commercial position. This decline accelerated after the conquests of Usman dan Fodio and the creation of the state of Maradi, whose surrounding country became a theater of combat and therefore less and less secure for the caravans. Also, trade was shifting away from Katsina, to some extent in favor of Kano, which became the principal point of convergence for trans-Saharan commerce. A number of Hausa and Tuareg merchants therefore left Katsina in order to reestablish themselves at Kano.[14]

The principal route that linked Kano to the Mediterranean ports passed through Ghadames, Ghat, Agadez, and Zinder, the latter a prosperous town in the nineteenth century because of its geographic location (Map 2.2). Its commercial role became important at a time when that of Maradi was modest to the point of nonexistence.

Zinder's Economic Reach

The sultanate of Damagaram at Zinder focused its activity on trans-Saharan trade, thereby attaining a considerable political and economic power, the sultans being able to take advantage of caravan traffic to provide their troops modern weapons capable of instilling fear and distrust in potential enemies. For example, Sultan Tanimoun, whose nineteenth-century reign marked the apogee of the Zinder sultanate, imported firearms from Tripoli and even manufactured his own cannon at local foundries.[15]

Military power allowed the Damagaram to extend its influence over a number of neighboring territories and their capitals: Mirriah, capital of the old state of Sossebaki; Gouré, capital of Minau; Kantché and Korgom,

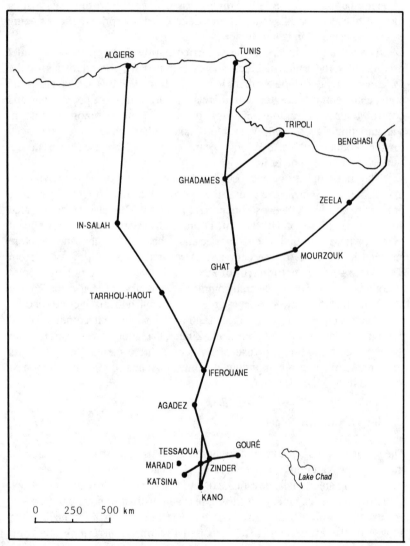

Map 2.2   Major Trans-Saharan Caravan Routes During the Nineteenth Century
Source: Adapted from Salifou, "Le Damagaram, ou sultanat de Zinder au XIXème siècle"

capitals of states of the same names; and Magaria were all annexed to Zinder. These towns also served as markets, satellites of the substantial market at Zinder.

Under the sultan's leadership, which was motivated by his interest in the arms trade that assured Zinder's hegemony, the town became a true commercial crossroads linking the Maghreb, the Hausa country, and the powerful state of Bornou. The principal merchants were the Arabs and the Toubous, often representing commercial houses in North Africa, including Tripoli, Murzuk, Ghadames, and Ghat.

Local Hausa merchants were less numerous, the most powerful being the very active chiefdom itself as well as a certain Malam Yaroh, who became as successful as the largest Arab businessman.[16] He established a commercial enterprise as effective in the countryside, where many peasants and artisans worked for him, as in the city. He had an agency in Tripoli and another in Kano. He maintained close relations with the Peul *sarkis* of Kano, Sokoto, Zaria, and Katsina, to whom he sold all sorts of products imported from the north.

In fact, the merchandise that fed the trans-Saharan trade was varied and extensive. The caravans arrived laden with European as well as Maghrebian products: blue and white cotton cloth, loaves of English sugar, cheap manufactures (paper, candles, etc.), blankets, plain and embroidered burnooses, and sabers from Tripoli. In exchange, they bore away tanned hides, ostrich plumes (especially during the second half of the century), leather goods, gum arabic, henna, and of course slaves, most of them destined for Cairo or Constantinople.

The trans-Saharan commerce ended with the arrival of the Europeans. Nevertheless, during the nineteenth century Zinder had acquired a commercial hegemony, profiting from its location as a way station on the route to Kano. At Zinder the caravans would disband, and the travelers, having nothing further to fear, would continue in small groups toward Kano. The decline of the route that terminated at Katsina favored Zinder; merchants who had been based at Tessaoua, located on the other route, moved to Zinder to continue their activities because the insecurity that existed at Tessaoua and Maradi was unfavorable to commerce.[17]

Maradi's Weak Economic Role

The situation at Maradi was quite different. The state of Maradi was usually at war until the end of the reign of Dan Baskore (1873). As this gave the region a reputation for insecurity, merchants were careful to avoid it. Further, as David notes, the rapacity of the *sarki* and their nobles was such that merchants and caravaners were discouraged from trying to enter the town to conduct business: "Strangers were robbed of their goods, pillaged shamelessly and . . . therefore never returned."[18] These depredations and the permanent state of war explain the negligible economic role Maradi played. Nonetheless, in a nearby village, Tarna, there existed a market that in a sense acted as Maradi's.

Tarna is an old village, founded earlier than Maradi by a man named Sarki Fulani Ditte. He arrived from the south in the company of several butchers from Katsina who quickly built up an important cattle market, then a general market (including, no doubt, slave trading). The existence of this market close to Maradi (less than 3 kilometers distant) may have made it unnecessary to build a market in the city proper. One might imagine it played a role similar to that of any *zongo* (a neighborhood on the outskirts of a town).

In the closing years of the nineteenth century, warfare against the Peuls became less frequent and the region of Maradi became more secure and attractive for the development of commerce. It was more and more frequently visited by small convoys of merchants shuttling between Maradi (that is, Tarna) and Tibiri, capital of Gobir, at one end, and Kano at the other. Such caravans would be directed by a *sarki*, the *madougou*, who would march at the head of the caravan and pay its taxes in the names of the merchants traveling with it. He would be chosen by virtue of his knowledge of the country and his ability to avoid its dangers.

At Maradi, the name that has remained preserved in legend is that of Madougou Waje. A native of Birni, he regularly led a caravan of numerous merchants who traveled by donkey to sell hides at Kano. They returned with cloth and cola nuts, some traveling all the way to the coast in order to procure these goods.[19] At the end of the nineteenth century, these small caravans constituted the main commercial traffic that affected Maradi and its region. They had neither the frequency nor the size of those that traveled by way of Zinder.

Finally, it is noteworthy that at Maradi there existed a certain number of artisanal corporations (*sana'a*), representing no doubt a mode of organization inherited from the traditions of Katsina. These corporations consisted of artisans belonging to the same occupational specialties, which demanded precise methods and technical knowledge. Chief among them were the smiths, dyers, weavers, tanners, potters, butchers, barbers, and *griots* (poet-musicians). These occupations were inherited and highly stratified, each having a *sarki*; within the community of producers there existed a socio-professional hierarchy highly respected among the population.

CONCLUSION

During the nineteenth century, the valley of the Maradi River became a place of refuge, a veritable entrenched camp where the Hausa who had escaped Peul domination could gather together. Maradi was thus more a town that filled up than one that grew. Its functions remained essentially political and military until the Europeans arrived. Its commercial activity was secondary, especially compared to that of a town such as Zinder: Maradi remained to one side of the great trans-Saharan currents, completely lacking a merchant tradition. Nowhere in its history is there any trace of great traders on the scale of Zinder's illustrious Malam Yaroh. Colonization would profoundly alter the roles and functions of these two towns.

NOTES

1. Philippe David, "Maradi, l'ancien Etat et l'ancienne ville: site, population, histoire," *Documents des Etudes Nigériennes*, No. 18, 1964.

2. The Anna were animists, politically unorganized and often itinerant.

3. David, "Maradi, l'ancien Etat et l'ancienne ville."

4. Sere de Rivières, *Histoire du Niger*.

5. They inflicted heavy taxes on the people, at times in kind (grain, livestock), and at times in cowrie shells, the local currency.

6. J. Tilho, *Documents scientifiques de la mission Tilho (1906–1909)*, Vol. 2 (Paris, 1910–1914). Cited by P. David.

7. The etymology of *Maradi* remains obscure and controversial.

8. M. G. Smith, "A Hausa Kingdom: Maradi under Dan Baskore, 1854–1875," in *West African Kingdoms in the Nineteenth Century*, ed. D. Forde and P. Kaberry (Oxford: Oxford University Press, 1967), pp. 93–122.

9. In the Hausa language, a *birni* is a neighborhood of dwellings built within a town, in contrast to a *zongo*, a neighborhood at the edge of a town.

10. Philippe David, "La geste du grand Kaura Assao," *Documents des Etudes Nigériennes*, No. 17, 1967.

11. J. Janvier, "Autour des missions Voulet-Chanoine en Afrique Occidentale," *Présence Africaine*, No. 22, October-November 1958.

12. J. F. Rolland, *Le Grand Capitaine: un aventurier inconnu de l'épopée coloniale* (Paris: Grasset, 1976).

13. In the Hausa country, the expedition was called *sara-sara*, the word *sara* meaning to chop wood into small fragments. [The Voulet-Chanoine column, two French officers commanding African troops, carried the routine violence of such expeditions to an extreme, becoming something of a rogue force. As word of their depredations spread, Colonel Klobb set out to head them off, taking with him French "regulars" rather than Africans—Translator.]

14. Usufu Bala Usman, "The Transformation of Katsina (1796–1903): The Overthrow of the Sarauta System and the Establishment and Evolution of the Emirate," Ph.D. dissertation, Ahmadu Bello University, 1974, pp. 466–469.

15. A. Salifou, "Le Damagram, ou sultanat de Zinder au XIXème siècle," *Documents des Etudes Nigériennes*, No. 27, 1971.

16. A. Salifou, "Malam Yaroh, un grand négociant du Soudan Central à la fin du XIXème siècle," *Journal de la Société des Africanistes*, 42, 1 (1972), pp. 7–27.

17. S. Baier, *An Economic History of Central Niger* (Oxford: Clarendon Press, 1980).

18. David, "Maradi: l'ancien Etat et l'ancienne ville."

19. P. E. Lovejoy, "The Kambarin Beriberi: The Transformation of a Specialized Group of Hausa Kola Traders in the Nineteenth Century," *Journal of African History*, 14, 4 (1974), pp. 633–652.

3

Colonial Maradi:
An Administrative Capital
Becomes Involved in Trade

ESTABLISHING COLONIAL POWER
AND A TRADE ECONOMY

Once the political borders had been clearly delineated with the British, who had taken possession of Nigeria, it took only a few years for the French to complete their domination of the chiefdoms, which found themselves despoiled of most of their powers. The colonial government quickly knitted together a network of administrative and military posts that allowed it to control the country and to seat its own authorities. Maradi was chosen to be an administrative post and then capital of a *cercle* (1927).[1]

By contrast, the transformation of the local economy and its adaptation to Western interests took longer: the advent of Europeans precipitated dislocations that were felt by the local population as an economic recession whose miseries continued until the end of World War I. Aware of the problems and judging that the Territory of Niger was lacking neither economic value nor attractions, the colonial government decided to stimulate the economy by introducing a new product, groundnuts, and by creating modern infrastructure, including communications. Situated at the center of one of Niger's best agricultural regions, Maradi benefited from these initiatives, becoming a small regional economic center as well as an administrative capital.

Creating the Frontier with Nigeria

The Europeans, driven by a desire to expand their territorial holdings, pushed ever deeper into the African continent, the French moving from west to east, the British from south to north. The rivalry between the two empires was intense, and in order to avoid military confrontation at the outward edges of the new territories, their diplomats met in Paris in 1898 to establish a treaty delimiting the frontiers between the future Niger and Nigeria.

This bit of geographic surgery, quite geometric on paper, followed a line between two towns: Say, on the Niger River south of Niamey, and Baroua, near Lake Chad. The Say-Baroua line awarded to the United Kingdom virtually all of what is today central Niger, including all the region of Maradi as well as most of Gobir. As a result, in 1902 a small British detachment led by Lieutenant Merrick traveled through the region as an act of sovereignty.

The French, after several reconnaissance missions, obtained British consent to important modifications to the border because the lands awarded to them were mostly desert and lacked economic potential. A new treaty, signed at London in 1904, shifted the Say-Baroua line to the south, giving France all of Gobir and a large part of the left bank of the Maradi River. This line was moved yet again toward the south at the second London conference (1906), and the new border was redrawn from one end to the other by a Franco-British expedition (Tilho-O'Shea), whose line was finally adopted at the London conference of January 31, 1910.[2] The states of Gobir and Maradi were integrated into the military Territory of Niger, and it was not until 1909 that the "first white man," Lieutenant Braive, arrived at Maradi.

The Administrative Outpost and Its Functions

Only after the London convention of 1906 was the French administrative network extended across eastern Niger to the shores of Lake Chad; thereafter, the entire region began to be administered from colonial outposts.

Maradi, well situated geographically and already the capital of a chiefdom, was chosen for construction of a post, situated upon the plateau in a position to dominate (in a real as well as figurative sense) the *birni*, the old city center founded by Dan Kassawa and fortified by Dan Baskore. The political, judicial, and administrative powers were withdrawn from the chiefdom and transferred to the *commandant*, Lieutenant Braive: France intended to exercise direct administrative control over the territory now under its authority. The former organization of Maradi, including its military role, was supplanted by new institutions: the *sarki*, whose will had been incontestible up until that point, found himself required to obey the orders of the local French commander.

Colonization also brought pacification and an end to warfare against the Peuls, who themselves had passed under British domination despite ferocious resistance, the taking of Sokoto and Katsina having been no easy task.

At the governmental level, Maradi steadily increased in influence: in 1901, the *commandant* of the region of Zinder signed a treaty of protection with the sultan of Tessaoua, Mijinyawa, who had been forced to flee Maradi and had founded at Tessaoua a small, independent principality. The installation of a French resident at Tessaoua, to whom was assigned control over the sultanate of Maradi, suggests that at an early stage the French military confused the relative importance of the two chiefdoms and their towns. This explains why Maradi was ruled from Tessaoua at the beginning, was merely part of the *cercle* of Madaoua from 1907 until 1921, and was rejoined to Tessaoua from 1921 until 1926 after having been redesignated a subdivision.

Overtaking Tessaoua in importance and finally dominating it, Maradi was chosen capital of the *cercle* by the decree of December 4, 1926, Tessaoua becoming a subdivision of the *cercle* of Maradi. At that point, a civilian administrator (a Monsieur Froger) took charge and the town began to fulfill new functions.

Administrative Functions

The transfer of the *cercle* capital in 1927 necessitated the construction of a certain number of buildings to house the colonial governmental apparatus. The residence of the *commandant de cercle* was completed in February 1927, just in time for the arrival of Froger; to it were added in turn the guardhouse, offices for various administrative services, and living quarters for the Europeans. However, Maradi became the base for only a small garrison, certainly unimportant in comparison with that stationed at Zinder, which had become the principal political and military center of the entire colony.

Judicial Functions

The decree of November 10, 1903, organized a system of justice under local law in French West Africa (Afrique Occidentale Française, or AOF), resting on three principles: respect for the customs of persons under the law, involvement of administrators in the execution of justice, and juridical control of decisions.

With regard to application of the decree, the governor general of the AOF provided the following instructions in 1905:

> I call your particular attention to the provisions of Article 75, under the terms of which indigenous justice applies local customs in every matter in which they are not contrary to the principles of French civilization.
>
> Indigenous courts are to judge either following quranic rules (Malekite rite), more or less modified by usage, as accepted in a large part of our territories, or following local traditions in those regions not yet under Muslim influence.
>
> We cannot impose upon our subjects those provisions of our French law that are manifestly incompatible with their social condition. However, we can no longer tolerate the use, in defiance of our authority, of certain customs contrary to our principles, to humanity, and to natural law.[3]

To conform to this spirit, traditional justice was administered at Maradi, but the decisions were controlled by the colonial government.

"Intellectual" Functions

In 1927 the first French educator was appointed to direct the modest school opened in 1912 by the interpreter Lobit; it had fifteen pupils, recruited among the children of chiefs and nobles.

At the end of the 1930s, Maradi had thus become a small seat of government. However, the economic objectives pursued under colonialism were to change the town even further.

Economic Consequences of the European Presence

Before examining in detail how the trading economy was put into practice, we should understand the economic consequences of the arrival of Europeans in this part of the Sahel. The regional economy was disrupted, affected in part by the decline of centuries-old trans-Saharan commerce, in part by the substitution of European for local money, and finally by the installation of a customs frontier along the border that had just been established.

The period of transformation of the economy and its adaptation to Western norms, criteria, and interests covers roughly the first two decades of the twentieth century. For the autochthonous peoples it was an era of crises and recessions aggravated by climatic conditions unfavorable to farming and herding. Whereas in the nineteenth century the region benefited from reasonably good natural conditions and experienced no prolonged droughts (except in 1855), the twentieth century began with a series of years in which rainfall was below normal.[4] The season 1913–1914 was marked by a severe famine (*kumumuwa*) that claimed many victims. It was in this context that the Europeans assured their economic dominion.

The Decline of Trans-Saharan Commerce

The vigorous caravan traffic that operated between the centers of North Africa and black Africa diminished progressively after 1900 for two principal reasons. First, the decline was certainly due to the growing insecurity that existed along its entire length: in the desert, caravans were attacked and stripped as early as 1895 (and definitely by 1899–1900) by bands of armed robbers, either Arabs or Toubous. Crossing the Aïr range became equally dangerous because groups of Tuareg opposed French control of their region. Similarly, in the Damergu, the conflicts that pitted the Tuareg Kel Ewey against the Imezureg became transformed into attacks against caravans in which merchants from Tripoli became the main victims.[5]

The second reason was economic: the cost of transporting merchandise imported or exported by sea via the south (that is, via present-day Nigeria) diminished considerably. It became less expensive than trans-Saharan transport because the British provided modern infrastructure, especially transport and communications, to their colony. The arrival of the railway at Kano in 1912 devastated the Saharan caravans (since rail transport costs were one-half to one-third of caravan costs), which were already being taxed by both colonial governments.

This difference in cost, combined with the insecurity of the convoys, was fatal to trans-Saharan trade, which decreased as the southern route prospered. Former Saharan "ports," such as Zinder, whose prosperity had depended upon their geographic advantages found themselves relegated to backwater status, declining in comparison with Lagos, Kano, and Katsina, which were served by ocean port facilities, railways, and roads suitable for motor traffic.[6]

However, the trans-Saharan trade diminished slowly, until there remained only the salt caravans (the *azalay*), conducted by the Tuareg, who supplied the oases far from Bilma and Fachi with millet, skins, and cloth and who returned with salt, natron, and dates.[7] These products were traded in the markets of Agadez, Zinder, and Maradi, as well as others across the border in Nigeria.

The Substitution of European for Local Money

The money that had circulated in the region consisted of cowries, small seashells imported from the Maldive Islands in the Indian Ocean. The cowries were supplemented by two silver coins imported from Europe via the desert: the French five-franc coin and the Austrian taler (engraved with an effigy of Empress Maria Theresa). At the beginning of the twentieth century, each coin was worth 5,000 cowries.

Out of self-interest, and as a matter of principle, the colonizers substituted their own currencies, the franc to the north of the Say-Baroua line and the pound to the south. Until 1910, the French colonial government accepted cowries in payment of various taxes; thereafter, only French currency would do. By 1908 the government had fixed the official exchange rate at 6,000 cowries per five-franc coin.

The shortage of coins in circulation (especially those of low face value, such as fifty-centime and one-franc coins, for which there was great demand) and the need to obtain them in order to pay taxes or conduct commerce encouraged development of a black market: the five-franc coin soon came to be exchanged at 7,000 cowries. This created opportunities for chiefs of cantons (who were responsible for tax collections), colonial officials, and local employees (such as foot soldiers), who received about one-third of their pay in small coins and who could engage in various speculations as a result. The black market worked against the local populations, who found their traditional money considerably devalued.[8] It continued until cowries were finally eliminated and replaced by the franc in general usage, undoubtedly by 1920.

Installation of the Customs Service

Collection of tariffs was preceded by the imposition of numerous other taxes that produced unpleasant effects. Until 1903, French fiscal policy consisted of taxing the different chiefdoms, on the theory that they were the summit of a fiscal hierarchy inasmuch as they levied individual taxes on their subjects and various other taxes on caravan commerce, marketplaces, and artisans. In taxing the chiefdoms, the government thought it was reaching the entire population indirectly.

In 1903 the French, assuming that the chiefdoms were enriching themselves excessively and arbitrarily, abolished the market taxes and the tolls charged caravans, only to reestablish them in 1906, this time, however, controlling them directly: merchants and artisans were required to pay an annual tax and often supplementary market taxes as well.

For example, livestock sales involved a tax ranging from 3 francs for each steer, horse, or camel sold, down to 55 centimes for each sheep or goat. This produced a shift of the livestock markets from Niger to the other side of the frontier, where they could be conducted freely.

The colonial government also instituted levies on caravan trade. This was easily accomplished where the Saharan trade was concerned because it used a limited number of routes, easily controlled. It was quite different with the numerous small donkey caravans that linked Maradi with Kano and Katsina, which used a multitude of trails.

With the pacification of the region, such commerce developed very rapidly at Maradi and for that matter throughout the military territory of Niger, which became sufficiently prosperous for the colonial government to establish customs posts all along the border with Nigeria (by order of the governor general of the AOF, November 6, 1913). The customs department created in 1913 comprised a bureau of customs, responsible for collection of duties on merchandise at entry and exit; two tax collection offices (at Nielloua and at Garin dan Sadao); and watch stations whose task it was to escort convoys to the tax collection offices. It was forbidden to enter the region of Maradi by any trails other than those leading to such stations, responsibility for which was largely confided to Senegalese soldiers.

The installation of this customs system produced disastrous consequences in the region and throughout the entire country. Prices rose to levels well above those in Nigeria. In addition, the importance of Nigerien markets close to the Nigerian border diminished, while that of markets south of the border increased. Worse, because of abuses and extortions by frontier guards, a number of merchants deserted the markets in Niger and emigrated to Nigeria.

The customs system aggravated the country's misery during the famine of 1914. Many inhabitants of the Maradi region fled to Nigeria in the hope of finding better conditions. In the face of such a catastrophe, the government became more flexible and put an end to the customs experiment (by order of the governor general of the AOF, February 1, 1918), which had been causing nothing but heartbreak for five years. The resulting economic morass led the government to modify its policies shortly after World War I.

Creating the Trade Economy

Conscious of the difficulties, aware that the region was falling behind the lands to the south administered by the British, and disquieted by the migratory movement toward Nigeria, the French government undertook a series of measures intended to stimulate the local economy. At Maradi, these involved creating new infrastructure. "Colonial commerce" also made its first appearance, with the arrival of various European commercial houses.

The Creation of Modern Infrastructure

At the beginning of the century, Maradi still possessed no marketplace, although there was one in the neighboring village of Tarna. The market at Tarna had begun as a place to sell cattle and slaves; taxes on livestock sales and the abolition of slavery and slave trading quickly reduced its influence, which shifted to the market at Djibya, in Nigeria.

In 1923 a decree announced the creation of a marketplace at Maradi itself, located at the base of the plateau between the African town and the administrative zone that overlooked it (see Map 1.6). In 1927 this site was abandoned and a new market was located on the west side of town on land occupied by the hamlet of Makoyo (or Jinjino Baka), part of which was torn down. The new market became a lively place as trade relocated there; the European companies and Lebanese merchants moved in bit by bit. Local merchants came there on Sunday, market day, to sell their products.

At that time Maradi's main trading partners were Kano and Katsina: for example, small convoys traveled to Kano, the merchants riding on the backs of donkeys laden with skins (the region's main export), and returning with cotton cloth and various products imported from Europe. They also visited the markets and villages in the bush, where they bought animals and grain for resale in Nigeria.

The accounts and recollections lead one to think that these small merchants were very active; the prosperity of some was indeed noteworthy. For example, Dan Guidi and Na Maka did business in cola nuts, traveling as far as Côte d'Ivoire for supplies; another merchant, known as Kaschalo, specialized in sales of cotton cloth and general merchandise; Bauchi, who was based at Tibiri, dealt in hides and skins, using buyers who circulated throughout the bush; and *Alhaji* Malam Nassaru did a diverse business, becoming in the process a supplier to retailers. By 1930 Malam Nassaru was one of the richest traders in town, but the flood of 1945 ruined him, as his home and warehouses were looted.

These minor commercial activities would continue to grow, commensurate with improvements in Maradi's links to the countryside and to other economic centers in the region. For example, beginning in 1921 it became possible for vehicles to reach Madaoua, Zinder, and Djibya. These improvements were carried out using requisitioned labor. The final touch came with installation of the first telephone line (1924) linking Maradi and Zinder. Maradi had at last become important enough to attract the European commercial houses.

Installation of European Commercial Houses

By providing infrastructure and communications, the colonial government's initiatives made Maradi not only an administrative but also a small commercial center. This attracted numerous firms and private traders to colonial commerce, which rapidly came to include control over distribution of European imports as well as commercialization of groundnuts, whose production the government was encouraging in order to revitalize the economy, especially after 1924. The first Europeans to enter commerce at Maradi were two Englishmen, Guarp and Hammond, who set up shop in 1914. These two had ambitious plans for importing cotton fabric from Europe and exporting skins, but their business soon failed.[9]

It was during the postwar recovery years (beginning in 1921–1922) that durable colonial commerce arrived with firms such as Gottanègre (1923) and Ambrosini (1925). They were followed much later (between 1934 and 1937) by branches of the large companies then spreading over much of Africa, such as the Compagnie du Niger Français (CNF), the Société Commerciale de l'Ouest Africain (SCOA), and the Compagnie Française de l'Afrique de l'Ouest (CFAO). These were extending commercial networks they had already established in Nigeria (CFAO had been there since 1904).

These large firms were characterized by the diversity and extent of their activities, facilitated by the substantial means at their disposal. They handled export of groundnuts and simultaneously provided consumer goods, from foodstuffs to everyday items, notably fabrics. Their headquarters generally were in France, their organization in Africa being very hierarchical and structured, with each country having a principal agency in the capital and several branches scattered among the major towns. In Niger, however, they created their first outposts at Maradi and Zinder, reaching Niamey only later.

Conclusion

Control of the region of Maradi and of Niger generally, except for the Tuareg country, posed no serious problems for France. Control of the local economy accompanied the gradual establishment of political dominion. In the space of two decades, Maradi, formerly the capital of a prestigious and rather warlike chiefdom, became a small administrative post with sufficient assets (a hinterland reasonably fit for agriculture, close proximity to Nigeria, ample population) to become a trading center. Although it lacked a commercial tradition, the town would become the focal point for groundnut production and trade in imports by virtue of the European firms, which took over all local commerce except that at the lowest levels, left to small traders of Levantine (Lebanese and Syrian) and African origin.

THE GROUNDNUT TRADE
DURING THE COLONIAL PERIOD

The European firms arrived as groundnut production was getting established. From Dosso in the west to Zinder in the east, the groundnut region in Niger extended nearly 1,000 kilometers along the frontier with Nigeria. To the north, it was limited more or less by the line marking 500 millimeters of annual rainfall.

Production increased steadily. World War II noticeably slowed its growth, but progress resumed in 1946, with output reaching constantly higher tonnages in the years that followed. Commercialization became so important that the colonial government became involved in business operations and organized the exportation of groundnuts to the metropole. Opération Hirondelle (Operation Swallow), as the effort came to be called, was an important development for Maradi. The city, situated at the heart of the Nigerien groundnut region, benefited from the many effects of the business. These were not only economic—construction of a groundnut oil pressing mill, commercial buildings, and new residential districts—but social as well: a group of African traders emerged, the *Alhazai*, who were very active and closely allied with the European firms.

Evolution of the Groundnut Trade

In contrast to Senegal, Niger did not become involved with large-scale groundnut agriculture until after World War II.

Groundnut Commerce Before World War II

Introduction and development of groundnut culture took place gradually in Niger. For a time, transport problems were a very difficult obstacle. In 1911, when Niger was reattached to French West Africa, the territory was quite isolated; the fastest route to the metropole proceeded up the Niger River to Koulikoro and thence by rail via Kayes to Saint-Louis in Senegal.

The completion of a rail link between Kano and Lagos (1912) encouraged Hausa merchants at Kano (who were soon joined by Greeks and

Levantines) to stimulate groundnut culture throughout northern Nigeria. Exports rose from an annual average of 8,200 metric tons between 1910 and 1914 to 41,300 metric tons for the period 1915–1919.[10]

This growth of groundnut production in the British colony extended into French territory. Beginning in 1924, the colonial government distributed improved seed, and in the course of the 1924–1925 harvest the regions of Maradi and Zinder exported 1,590 metric tons of shelled groundnuts, carried on the backs of camels to Kano or Kaura Namoda for loading onto the trains.

In 1927 the government extended its efforts to the entire colony. Success produced an embryonic commercial network—by 1931 eleven trading firms were involved in the groundnut business. These trends were soon reversed; for one thing, the 1931 harvest was very poor because the Maradi region experienced a terrible drought (the El Gomma famine), and, for another, the worldwide Great Depression was raging in Europe, pushing down groundnut prices, which fell by half between 1928 and 1932. The merchants lost interest in a product that the cost of transport made unprofitable. Production fell, and producers began to consume their crops on the farm.

The business climate began improving in 1934, helping the regions of Maradi and Magaria (a town in the south of the *département* of Zinder), which now became major centers for the trade. Production continued to increase up to the beginning of World War II (except for the harvests of 1934–1935 and 1938–1939, when the crop volumes were poor) and attained new records: 45,000 metric tons exported during 1935–1936, for example.

World War II halted the expansion; the occupation of the French metropole by Germany, plus the lack of ships, left Niger completely isolated. As exports to France declined, they shifted to Nigeria: the French authorities sold the entire harvest of 1943–1944, except for a tiny amount reserved for the oil mill at Maradi, to Britain. Trading firms that had agencies on both sides of the frontier were chosen to export the crop; they arranged for transport and all customs formalities. The transactions took place in the frontier markets at Maradi, Matameye, Magaria, Dungass, and Sassoumbouroum.

Despite the problems, by the end of the 1930s, the French government had achieved its objective, which was to revitalize an economy that had been severely depressed at the end of World War I and to introduce a new product for which the metropole had a need.

The Groundnut Business Just After World War II

After having stagnated during the war, groundnut commerce resumed with the 1946–1947 harvest. The prewar records were reached and then surpassed. This intense development of groundnut cultivation was, from its inception, closely related to the peasants' need to obtain cash with which to pay their taxes.[11] This was the "motor" that drove the introduction and spread of groundnut cultivation to the point where it competed with production of millet, the staple of the local diet.[12]

The producers had to reconcile two imperatives: to feed themselves on the one hand and to pay the tax and buy necessities on the other.[13] Nevertheless, as Raynaut points out, the fiscal demands on rural communities did not stop growing, and this required the farmers to keep increasing the area planted in groundnuts in order to pay the ever heavier taxes: "As a result, whereas in 1952 each individual had to sell twenty-four kilograms of shelled groundnuts (at 16 CFA francs per kilogram) in order to pay the personal tax, by 1963 the amount had risen to forty kilograms (at 24 CFA francs per kilogram)."[14] Under the circumstances, it is not surprising that production rose so much and that by the eve of independence Niger was the second largest groundnut exporter in French West Africa.

The spectacular growth can also be explained by a measure taken at the beginning of the 1954–1955 growing season. The French government decided, in effect, to guarantee the purchase of a portion of Niger's groundnut crop at prices higher than the world market price. For all of Niger, marketed tonnage increased from 11,392 metric tons in 1950 to more than 100,000 in 1957–1958, and then declined (because of poor rainfall) to 62,500 in 1961–1962, the last year of the "traditional" groundnut business.

Finally, the frontier separating Niger from Nigeria posed a continuing problem, inasmuch as there were no natural or social obstacles (given that the populations on both sides shared a single language and culture) to reinforce it. The existence of innumerable trails across it made access easy and control very difficult. The participation of the two countries in different monetary zones encouraged traders to take advantage of local market conditions and to speculate in exchange rate fluctuations.[15] Until the end of World War II, therefore, a part of the Nigerien harvest was marketed in Nigerian towns close to the frontier. During the late 1940s and early 1950s, trade flowed first one way, then another.[16] From 1954 on, the French price guarantee at a level above world markets (and thus above that in Nigeria) stabilized the situation, and significant tonnages of Nigerian groundnuts (around 10,000 metric tons in 1955–1956) found their way into Niger. The franc devaluations of 1957 and 1958 changed the situation yet again, and as of 1960 there was near parity in price, with Nigeria holding a slight advantage and thus attracting a disproportionate share.

Organization of the Groundnut Trade

As in Senegal and Nigeria, the groundnut trade (*fulotin gujya*) provided a considerable stimulus to commerce in Niger's producing regions. As Nicolas notes, this was a time of celebration and plenty.[17] The trade was controlled by the European trading houses, which had a monopoly on groundnut exports. In addition, the colonial government imposed strict regulation and intervened to speed transport to the metropole.

Regulation of the Trade

The colonial authorities, which at the beginning were content just to encourage production indirectly through taxes and directly by distributing seed to the *sociétés de prévoyance* (provident societies), intervened more and more in the groundnut industry and imposed a regulatory system based upon that in Senegal. This system fixed time (fifteen weeks a year) and space limitations on business operations; the government decided opening and closing dates for the campaign and listed trading centers outside of which commercial operations were forbidden.[18]

During the 1960–1961 season, six trading points existed within the *cercle* of Maradi: Guidan-Roumji, Maradi, Madarounfa, Dan Issa, Tibiri, and Sabon Machi. The *cercle* of Tessaoua had four: Tessaoua, Gazaoua, Tchadaoua, and Gabaouri. To conclude a sale anywhere other than at these markets risked seizure of the product. These trading points were chosen on the basis of their geographic location, particularly ease of access; thus, they tended to be at major crossroads, which became small, bustling villages during the trading season.

Also, the regulations obliged each exporter to make an annual request to the *commandant de cercle* for authorization to participate in the trade, including a declaration of the number of sacks of groundnuts in the firm's possession. Only traders or buyers working with exporters were allowed to take part in the market.

The regulations were intended to protect producers against abuses and render them less dependent upon fluctuations in world market prices (hence the purchase price guarantee from 1954 on). In addition to the establishment of this legislation, the government also helped organize transportation, a crucial problem in landlocked countries like Niger.

Organization of Transport

From the beginning of the groundnut export business in Niger, the most practical route went through Nigeria. In regions such as those around Maradi and Zinder, this route was the shortest and best equipped in terms of infrastructure. Until the time just before World War II when trucks became the general means of transport, groundnuts were often sent to Kano and Kaura Namoda by camel or donkey. The latter remained in use up until 1953, when Opération Hirondelle was launched; this was a scheme to make sure that a major portion of Niger's groundnut crop would be exported through Cotonou, with the vehicles to be used for carrying merchandise imports on the return trip. It depended upon use of the Zinder-Parakou road and then the railroad from Parakou to Cotonou.

Such a major shift was undertaken primarily because of increasing delays encountered in moving the groundnut shipments to Lagos via Nigerian Railways. At times this meant delays of several months at Kano, waiting for railroad cars, during which time the groundnuts deteriorated because of acidification. In addition, the shift allowed a considerable savings in foreign exchange and facilitated loans by the Fond d'Investissement pour le Développement Economique et Social (FIDES, a French government agency) for improvements to the main road between Zinder and Parakou and for construction of a bridge across the Niger River at Malanville.

The new transportation scheme posed many difficulties, notably at the level of organizing commerce. Transport also appears to have been more expensive via Dahomey than via Nigeria. Nevertheless, until independence Opération Hirondelle carried heavy tonnages and represented an important savings in foreign exchange.

The Development of the Trade

The colonial government encouraged the commercial firms to establish offices at Maradi and to become involved in the groundnut trade. During the 1930s, the CFAO, CNF, and the SCOA had opened branches there. The European firms constituted the most powerful commercial interests in that they controlled the commercialization of groundnuts and the distribution of manufactured goods. Their main characteristics were diversity and extended influence, facilitated by the vast means at their disposal: they met the material needs of the groundnut harvest (balance scales, bags, trucks) and advanced funds or credit to their intermediaries.

In order to reach the producer, they resorted to numerous intermediaries who crisscrossed the pathways into the bush. At the very beginning of the groundnut business around Maradi they hired Nigerians who were familiar with the trade because it had already been operating for some years in Nigeria. Every morning (in some cases every week) they provided each intermediary a sum of money, receiving upon the intermediary's return a quantity of groundnuts, for which they paid a commission. Aside from these Nigerians, a Lebanese (Elias Issa) and an Arab (Bel Abd) also worked for the import-export houses and helped to train Nigeriens in the business. These rapidly took the Nigerians' places: the first "buyer" native to Maradi was *Alhaji* Daouda, who was a simple meat merchant when Elias Issa first hired him in 1935.

The launching of production and commercialization led to modifications in the trade. The large commercial firms delegated more and more of their marketing operations to independent traders, preferring to deal with only a few individuals whom they knew well. The traders received credit from the exporter at the beginning of the campaign (or in some cases every week), which they used to buy groundnuts, and were paid commissions at the end of the season.

The traders had teams of buyers who made purchases on local markets.[19] These buyers were most often recruited from among the local aristocracy or traditional merchants. The trader or exporter drew up an agreement in order to obtain a buyer's license from the government and authorization to use a "plot" in the market, paved with *banco* or cement and enclosed by low walls, in which the groundnuts were stored. Before World War II, such buyers fanned out into the bush markets with camels and donkeys, buying groundnuts.

As cultivation expanded, European and Lebanese merchants, especially those based at Kano, saw opportunities for fruitful business and arrived at Maradi to take part in the market. They moved vigorously to acquire groundnuts at the expense of the other exporters, and competition among the various buyers became very lively. This competition led the colonial government, under pressure from the import-export houses, to regulate the trade. It also led to the development of a market in which buyers encouraged groundnut production and sought to wrest it from their competitors by steering business toward one firm's market stall and away from another's, trying all the while to avoid provoking price cuts in retaliation. The solution, which arose spontaneously out of a social milieu that fortunately already existed, was the creation of permanent buying networks linking producers to buyers through a hierarchy of intermediaries.[20]

These buying networks also became involved in the distribution of manufactured goods imported by the commercial houses; the networks thus became true economic circuits. They incorporated highly structured, traditional social links, in particular that of patron and client. This relationship plays a large role in Hausa social structure. It consists of a link of dependence, freely established, between a "master" called "the father of the house" (*uban-gida*), and a "servant" or dependent (*bara*, plural *barori*). Servants put themselves at the service of the master, or patron, and render him multiple services without expecting any remuneration. In exchange, the patron is obliged to offer his dependents gifts, often expensive ones. The distinctive quality of this relationship is that the economic ties linking the two are less important than social or affective ties. The *bara* often obtains a certain prestige because of the link to the *uban-gida* and may even have numerous *barori* dependents himself.

The *bara* to *uban-gida* relationship assured cohesiveness in its networks and, by reason of its successive hierarchical levels, made it possible to link the commercial houses with the farmers. An important patron (trader, buyer) would have numerous dependents who themselves would go out to buy groundnuts from the farmers, or who would do so through the intermediary of their own dependents. The economic weight of a given individual was thus related to social importance, to "richness in men" (*arzikin mutane*). The maintenance of the social network created even more economic power, which in turn made it necessary for patrons to redistribute a part of their own wealth among their.dependents.

The different dependents, often chosen among the influential persons in each village, prepared for the annual trading cycle by distributing cash advances and gifts to producers in order to link them to specific buyers. These gifts and advances were frequently distributed during the growing season (July, August, and September) when farmers needed money, the previous harvest having been consumed and the next harvest not yet having taken place.

This system of recruiting was used to organize the annual trade beforehand, the leaders (*madugou*) playing an important role in the service of the buyers, whose principal task was reduced to that of weighing the crop.[21] In practice, it was difficult to strengthen the dependence of the seller upon the buyer, inasmuch as there were extensive networks of intermediaries in the bush, who were much solicited by the traders and exporters and who changed employers frequently.

The organization just described (Figure 3.1) and its commercial hierarchy (Figure 3.2) existed until 1962, when the government of Niger decided to restructure the commercial system.

On the eve of independence, the principal groundnut exporters in the *cercle* of Maradi were

- foreign firms: CNF, the CFAO, and the SCOA;
- local Europeans: B. Ruetsch, Dumoulin, and Cogeac;
- Levantines: the Assad, Abed, Elias Issa, *Alhaji* Ali, and Khalil Azard families;
- a special case: the vegetable oil milling company Société Industrielle et Commerciale du Niger (Siconiger), which in 1950 created its own network of buyers (it had previously bought from the foreign import-export firms) to obtain groundnuts directly from the local markets. The oil was exported to France.

According to the archives of the colonial revenue service for 1959, fifty-eight traders operated in the Maradi region for the exporters just listed, obtaining groundnuts through 190 buyers, who represented about a quarter of the licensed buyers operating in Niger.

Effects of the Trade

The Economic Results

The groundnut trade set in motion other types of commerce and stimulated the growth of Maradi.

Commerce in manufactured products. The sale of imported manufactures was closely related to groundnut trade, which opened new outlets for industries in the metropole.[22] In addition, it allowed the European firms to spread their risks and eventually to cover losses in the commercialization of groundnuts, due to drought, for example. As soon as they were established, the

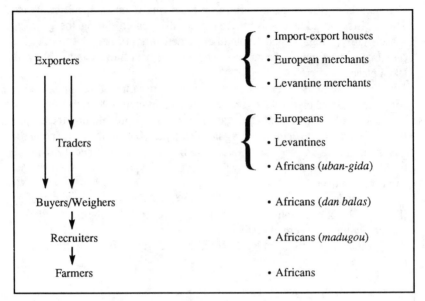

Figure 3.1   Organization of Groundnut Procurement

import-export houses opened retail outlets in which they sold all kinds of consumer goods: foodstuffs (sugar, rice, salt, flour, tomatoes, crackers, etc.), trade items (luggage, oil lamps, cooking pots, bowls, cigarettes, etc.), fabrics (canvas, percale), and, later, construction materials (cement, iron, tools, etc.).

The stocking of their branches was usually accomplished as a counterpoint to groundnut exports; thus, the objectives of Opération Hirondelle were not only the transport of groundnuts toward Cotonou but also the import of industrial products into Niger (see Table 3.1). For importing "upstream," the commercial route was the same as that for groundnuts.[23] Selling "downstream," the distribution of these products in the bush was carried out through the same channels as those used to collect the groundnuts, the network described above playing an essential role and transactions being conducted in both directions, groundnuts going one way and manufactured goods the other.

The trade in European products existed throughout the year but was brisk after the sale of the harvest, the numerous peddlers (most often groundnut buyers or recruiters) profiting from the bit of money the farmers had left over, which they spent on cloth, perfumes, and other goods.

All commerce, including that involving groundnuts, depended upon the availability of credit; the import-export houses extended advances to traders

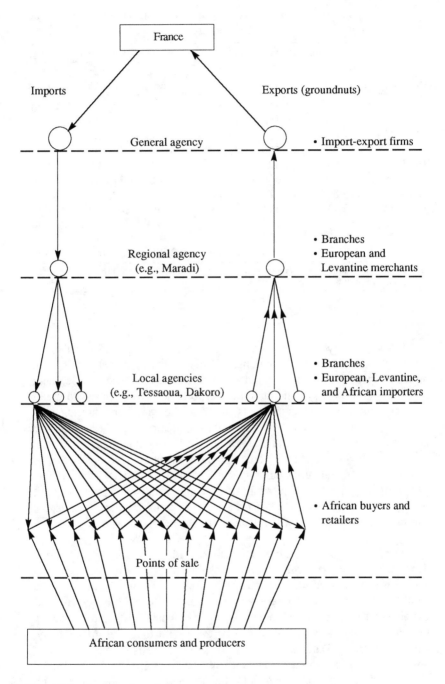

Figure 3.2   Organization of the Trading Economy

Table 3.1   Opération Hirondelle Incoming and Outgoing Freight Tonnages in Niger

	Imports via Dahomey			Groundnut Exports via Dahomey		
Harvests	West	East Central	Total	West	East Central	Total
1953–54	—	4,470	4,470	—	4,700	4,700
1954–55	5,000	6,150	11,150	—	12,350	12,350
1955–56	7,000	10,000	17,000	6,000	18,000	24,000
1956–57	14,000	13,500	27,500	6,500	20,200	26,700
1957–58	11,489	10,827	22,316	9,060	19,600	28,600
1958–59	8,400	13,000	21,400	8,600	17,500	26,100
1959–60	13,604	12,175	25,779	3,222	19,364	22,586
1960–61	16,117	12,571	28,688	5,641	23,650	29,291
1961–62	13,845	11,035	24,880	4,083	22,377	26,460
1962–63	16,682	10,700	27,382	4,432	21,540	25,972
1963–64	19,178	6,866	26,044	2,901	21,467	24,368

Source: Banque centrale des Etats de l'Afrique de l'Ouest, Document No. 116 of March 1965, reported in Pehaut, *L'archide au Niger*

and buyers so they could buy groundnuts from the farmers. Similarly, the firms provided advances for purchase of manufactures, which funds were repaid after the goods were sold. In order to finance each year's cycle, these firms turned to banks in the metropole or to local banks. Access to credit was very important to all participants, including the traders and buyers.

Commercial networks had important implications for the towns. The European houses sold in wholesale or quasi-wholesale amounts to African intermediaries, who in turn offered the goods at retail. The intermediaries were numerous and often quite specialized with regard to product line. Generally, they paid cash for a part of their merchandise, receiving the rest on credit. The shopkeepers often had networks of retailers outside the central market who sold all over town and at the markets in nearby bush villages.

The trade in fabric was typical of this kind of commerce. *Alhaji* Maman dan Dano, one of the town's major merchants, had as his retailers (*barori*) several men who have since become senior *Alhazai*. During the mornings he would turn over to them a variety of merchandise (cloth, various kinds of clothing, perfume, etc.), and in the evening they would bring him the money they had earned; he would then reward them with food and gifts. Today, *Alhaji* Maman dan Dano is very old and has retired.[24] His former *barori* now do business on their own accounts, thanks to large gifts from the *Alhaji*, who helped them go into business for themselves. Now major businessmen in their own right, they visit him regularly, bringing gifts as a way of showing their awareness of a permanent debt of gratitude for his having taught them business skills and having provided them means to go into business. Relationships of this kind among the Hausa merchants in the Zongo quarter of Lomé have been analyzed by Michel Agier.[25]

Commerce in hides and skins. Hides and skins have been traded around Maradi since ancient times; for a very long time, goat hides were sent to market at Kano and then exported to a world market that knew them as "Kano-Sokoto" products.

The colonial government, aware that the abundant russet goats provided high-quality raw material, intervened in the trade and forbade exports to Nigeria. Nevertheless, it encouraged the commercial houses to get involved in collecting and exporting skins by air from Maradi to the metropole and other countries. Several firms soon became involved in the new activity, including Siconiger, CFAO, and CNF. CNF was an affiliate of the United African Company (active throughout the former British colonies), which in turn was part of Unilever, one of the world's largest leather-processing companies. Hides could be collected at the same time as groundnuts, but collecting generally took place during the slack period after the harvest. The market was informal, the firms using their networks of groundnut buyers; for example, *Alhaji* Daouda bought groundnuts for Siconiger and hides for the Union Commerciale du Niger (UNC, a Siconiger subsidiary created to enter the hides and skins business), thanks to the many intermediaries he had in markets scattered throughout the bush.

This business required closer attention than the buying of groundnuts. Certain merchants, paying scant regard to the quality of what they were buying, quickly got into trouble. For this reason the trade became the preserve of a few specialists, notably *Alhaji* Mati and *Alhaji* Yawa. Credit practices based upon those used in the groundnut business linked the dealers to the large import-export houses.

Maradi became a center for this commercial activity as well, and companies such as the UNC grew steadily until 1970, when the local tannery opened, making Maradi a focal point of Niger's leather industry.

Commerce in cola nuts. A very traditional business, cola-nut marketing was scarcely affected by the groundnut trade but remained in the hands of African specialists: *colatiers* have to know their delicate activity extremely well, since cola nuts do not last unless they remain moist (otherwise they are said to "burn"), which requires a great deal of care.

According to numerous informants, on the eve of World War II this business was synonymous with one of the first great *Alhazai* of Maradi, Gambo Maigoro.[26] *Alhaji* Gambo Maigoro was from Kano and originally came to Maradi to participate in the groundnut trade. Contrary to the habit of most Nigerians, who usually came during the trading season and returned home at the end of it, *Alhaji* Gambo Maigoro took up residence at Maradi.

For several years, he was a groundnut buyer for the Levantine trader Elias Issa. At the end of the trading season he would travel to Kano with the donkey caravans in order to buy cola nuts, which he resold at wholesale, discount, and retail. As trade relations with Nigeria increased in number and speed thanks to increasing use of trucks, he intensified his activities and developed close ties with his suppliers in Kano.[27]

This organization of the cola trade lasted until the mid-1950s, at which point the British pound circulating in Nigeria became much stronger than the French franc, which was devalued twice, in 1957 and again in 1958. Cola nuts from Nigeria became more and more expensive, leading *Alhaji* Gambo Maigoro to turn to suppliers located in the franc zone in order to avoid the foreign exchange problem. This is how Ivorian and, above all, Voltaic merchants from Bobo Dioulasso replaced the Nigerians and how the western cola nut supplanted that from the south.

At Maradi, such merchants had only *Alhaji* Gambo Maigoro to represent them, and the scale of his business expanded until, as one informant puts it, "today not a single cola nut fails to pass through his hands." In addition, he bought several trucks, and although he abandoned his role of buyer in the groundnut trade, he still participated in Opération Hirondelle to reap the benefits offered to local transportation companies.

His cola business rested upon a very hierarchical structure of retailers living in the main towns, individuals who themselves used networks of smaller retailers who covered the bush villages, supplying the entire region. In town, he supplied two wholesalers who had their own extensive commercial networks.[28]

Alhaji Gambo Maigoro put his main efforts into cola nuts, but he did not neglect other revenue opportunities.[29] Since his death, the cola business has been controlled by two men who had been his subordinates.[30] They buy their western cola nuts at Niamey because the Voltaic merchants no longer visit Maradi but sell their goods at Niamey as soon as they have cleared customs.

Urban development. Before World War II, Maradi was no more than a little crossroads, less important than Zinder, where the colonial trade was also located. The groundnut trade and the various enterprises related to it did not really make themselves felt until after the reconstruction years, 1945 and later into the 1950s, at which time they became the principal focus of Nigerien commerce.

Maradi, therefore, became a collecting and transfer point for groundnuts and skins, as well as the point of departure for distribution of manufactured goods into the nearby bush. As a result, its influence over the neighborhood increased and its own activities became totally oriented toward that area. During the dry season (October to May), its commercial activities attracted many farmers seeking temporary employment. For one thing, the groundnut trade created employment (for market porters, loaders for the trucks, etc.), and for another the vegetable oil mill, which used many laborers, increased its productive capacity during the 1950s. Rural workers would return to their villages as the rainy season approached in order to prepare their fields. Nevertheless, from about 1955 on a certain number settled in the town.

The takeoff of commercial groundnut production affected other activities; for example, Maradi, as one of the major centers for Opération Hirondelle, became the headquarters for numerous European and African transport services. The construction industry, stimulated by the rebuilding that took place after the flood, attracted several small European businesses. The increase in African business activity (by petty traders, artisans, and others) added considerable life to the local scene.

Maradi, capital of the local *cercle*, became more and more of an administrative center as the colonial government expanded. It became the headquarters for schools, public health (hospital, dispensaries, maternity services), and culture (cinema), each of which offered its own attractions to people in the countryside.

Social Effects

The European firms were at the summit of a highly structured commercial hierarchy, working through various agents to buy groundnuts and sell manufactured goods. These agents became indispensable intermediaries between the commercial houses and the producers. African and Levantine traders saw opportunities for profit in this situation; the latter increasingly constituted a small, privileged group at the center of local society.

Levantine commerce. Arriving at Maradi in 1935, Elias Issa became one of the first groundnut buyers for the commercial houses. He and most other Levantine merchants came from Kano, extending commercial circuits that they had established in Nigeria. They usually served as intermediaries between European distributors and Africans engaged in retailing, in which they also dabbled at times. They received large sums of money that permitted them to effect profitable transactions for the Europeans, yielding profits also for their own accounts. Access to bank credit gave them the means to go into business for themselves and to build volume. As a result, some made the transition from simple agent to exporter, later becoming distributors following the creation of Sonara.[31] Finally, it must be emphasized that the Levantine merchants were usually better connected with African merchants (most spoke fluent Hausa, for example) than were the Europeans, and they were the financial power behind the success of quite a few *Alhazai*.

African commerce. The number of local merchants participating in the groundnut trade was directly proportional to the growth in groundnut cultivation. Most often, they were buyers who circulated among the farmers, buying for the accounts of Levantine or French merchants. A few became traders directly with the import-export companies.[32]

Some African merchants abused their positions as buyers, notably their access to credit, in order to enrich themselves. Credit is a very old institution in Hausa society, linked to the agricultural cycle.[33] Farmers frequently borrow when supplies are short and repay at the harvest. The practice of lending in kind (millet) or in cash was also widespread. Buyers extended loans for short periods (three or four months) and at very high rates (100 percent or more). On balance, the farmers were almost always the losers, since at the time of repayment the buyers engaged in various maneuvers at their expense: purchase of the harvest at low prices before the official commencement of trade, speculation on the price of millet (buying at low prices during the harvest in order resell at high prices during periods of shortage), and so on.

These credit practices undoubtedly benefited certain merchants who had capital, and they became an important method for accumulating more. In addition, they lent a certain cohesion to the commercial networks operated by the European companies, tightly linking the farmers at the bottom of the scale to specific intermediaries and, through them, to the companies.

The key practice of these commercial networks was very expensive for both exporters and buyers, for the scheme used credits and gifts as incentives for farmers. Prior to the trading season the buyers sought sizable credits in cash and merchandise at modest interest rates. Thus, the buyers were usually indebted for large sums of money to the commercial houses they represented, largely because of poor management and their practice of making ostentatious gifts.[34] Since the buyers had no other financial backers, the exporters and traders were often obliged to carry them in the hope of recovering their loans.[35] They sometimes had to resort to direct deductions from commissions owed to buyers. This is why they were more often successful with the sale of manufactures than with the collection of groundnuts.[36]

Nonetheless, among the traders and certainly among the many African buyers, few—at most a dozen—developed their business activity to any significant scale or commercial creditworthiness.[37] One may consider that these were the first, core members of the *Alhazai* merchant class in Maradi, whose activities were encouraged by the government of Niger following independence and whose numbers grew during the 1970s as a result of trade with Nigeria.

In 1960 their principal activity was the collection of groundnuts and the distribution of European goods in the bush. At the same time, most of them invested in transportation (by purchasing trucks), construction (notably in the Sabon Gari quarter that they built in Maradi), and in other commercial activities (hides and skins, cola nuts, etc.).

Biography of a wealthy groundnut merchant in Maradi. As an illustration of this first generation of major merchants, it is possible to sketch the life of one of them.[38]

Alhaji Ousmane, born at Tibiri (near Maradi), attended a quranic school for a number of years. At about age fifteen he arrived at Maradi, where he found work as a laborer at the Sudan Interior Mission, an organization run by US Protestants, which was constructing buildings on the west side of the old town. When that project was completed, the mission kept him on as a cook and then as a guard. From his contact with the missionaries, he learned to read and write, and his job as a guard allowed him to develop a small business on the side, selling paper and books, which rapidly diversified into other products (sugar, salt, etc.).

After the flood and the resulting transfer of the town to higher ground, he left his job at the mission and devoted himself to commerce, at which he prospered. *Alhaji* Ousmane supplied several other merchants with various items that they resold in the bush; thus, he became a source for other retailers.

Having earned a reputation for honesty, he became a groundnut buyer for Elias Issa, remaining with him for three or four years, during which he became thoroughly familiar with the groundnut trade. Building a good network of intermediaries in the bush (at Tibiri, Madarounfa, Dan Issa, Guidan-Roumji, Sabon Machi, Gazaoua, and Tchadaoua), he attracted notice at CNF, which made him a groundnut buyer and distributor of merchandise, which he handled through his bush retailers. As his business continued to grow, CNF sold him a truck on credit, which he repaid out of his groundnut trade.[39] This helped his business to expand again: he also became a groundnut buyer for the oil mill owned by Siconiger.

By the time the state company for groundnut marketing, the Société Nigérienne de Commercialisation de l'Arachide (Sonara), was created in 1962, *Alhaji* Ousmane was one of the five principal *Alhazai* of Maradi. With support from one of the local banks, he gained sufficient financial means to become an *organisme-stockeur* for and a minority shareholder in the new state firm.[40] Since Sonara did not import manufactured goods, he tentatively abandoned that branch of commerce in order to do nothing but buy groundnuts. He concentrated on groundnut buying throughout the 1960s but found his activities more and more hampered by state enterprises such as the Union Nigérienne de Crédit et de Coopération (UNCC) and the Société de Commerce et de Production du Niger (Copro-Niger), which the government created and relentlessly favored during the major drought (1973) that marked the decline of groundnut production in the region.

Alhaji Ousmane has thus found himself forced to reorient his activities. He has accumulated very large real estate holdings near Guidan-Roumji and has intensified his interest in millet and sorghum farming, for which he employs a large labor force and considerable farm equipment. He markets his harvest at the end of the dry season, a time of year when prices are at their highest, producing a substantial revenue. Although he was one of the principal *Alhazai* in Maradi at the beginning of the 1960s, he has seen his activity decline with the collapse of the groundnut trade, despite his efforts to diversify, especially into construction and transport. Even though his farms generate a large revenue, he does not figure today among the most prosperous of the *Alhazai*, whose fortunes usually are based on activities other than groundnut trade.

Conclusion

The groundnut trade and its ancillary activities (transport, oil milling, etc.) made Maradi a small regional center whose economy was oriented entirely toward its surrounding countryside. Still relatively unpopulated at the time of independence (12,500 inhabitants in 1959), it was the third largest town in Niger after Niamey (about 29,000) and Zinder (more than 22,000), which had been deprived of its administrative role in favor of Niamey.

The establishment and growth of the groundnut trade economy, however, permitted several African merchants to become wealthy and to achieve a scope of business based in large part on the importance of their commercial networks: "richness in men" is one of the pillars of their economic prosperity.[41] Among these first *Alhazai* we record the names of *Alhaji* Gambo Maigoro, *Alhaji* Daouda, *Alhaji* Nabangui, *Alhaji* Nayaché, *Alhaji* Maman Zinder, *Alhaji* Hanounou Coulibaly, Baba Madrounfa, and *Alhaji* Tella. Their success was already abundantly clear in 1960 inasmuch as their prestige among the population was considerable and a fraction of their income was redistributed via expensive gifts (closely regulated by custom) and sumptuous spending.

It must be emphasized that the expansion of this African commerce was encouraged by the traditional chiefdom of Maradi, which served as a mover and participant in the process. The traditional *sarki* at the time, *Alhaji* Mahaman Sani dan Zambadi Buzu, was himself a groundnut buyer, and quite a number of nobles participated in the trade or in the different occupations that served it. For example, the *maradi*, an official whose earlier function had been to oversee tax collections for the *sarki*, was also a longtime participant in the groundnut trade.

During the colonial epoch, African merchants were only intermediaries between the farmers and the commercial firms, which used them to improve their revenues from the trade. The government of the Republic of Niger provided new opportunities to the Africans when it decided, soon after taking power, to reform the commercial system that had been put in place during the colonial period. These reforms would profoundly change the basis of commerce at the local level.

STRUCTURAL REFORMS FOLLOWING INDEPENDENCE

Niger's independence set in motion a new state and put into place a political and bureaucratic bourgeoisie that gradually gathered the reins of government into its own hands. Even though there was no sharp organizational break with the structures of the colonial period, it is still essential to note that the new leaders of the country took a series of decisions, especially economic decisions, that would secure Niger's hold over the greater part of its own resources.

For example, the first president of the republic, Diori Hamani, told an audience at the Chamber of Commerce, Agriculture, and Industry of Niger at Niamey on October 19, 1961, that "political independence is consolidated by economic independence," and then added that

> the trade economy, which generates vast illicit profits and costs incompatible with modern economic life, is forever condemned. It is a vestige of a colonial past whose persistence is anachronistic in an independent country seeking development within the framework of a planned economy. The establishment of a modern, rational market structure has become an ineluctable necessity in order to safeguard the country's economic future.

Given this perspective, in 1962 the Nigerien government began creating state enterprises in order to purify the commercial system—notably groundnut marketing and distribution of imports—and to control them closely. These reforms had inevitable consequences on various economic actors, for example, prompting a retreat from vast sectors of the economy by the European commercial houses. In addition, the restructuring of markets was accompanied by systematic organization of the rural masses, involving new cooperatives and credit mechanisms.

Niger's independence occurred under favorable economic circumstances: its first decade was marked by unprecedented results in groundnut production, the country's principal cash earner. This very strong market had repercussions on the evolution of Maradi, which by the time of the great drought had grown from a colonial trading post to a small regional capital exercising an increasing attraction on its surrounding region.

Creation of State Organizations

Two new commercial institutions were established: Sonara for the marketing of groundnuts, and Copro-Niger for the sale of manufactured goods and the purchase of foodstuffs. Aside from the reorganization of commercial networks, the Nigerien government needed to resolve the problem posed by Opération Hirondelle and determine its future. As for organizing the rural population into cooperatives, the UNCC replaced precursor or para-cooperative institutions of the colonial period (provident societies and rural mutual development societies); its objective was to help the farmers to commercialize their own crops and to involve them in efforts to modernize agricultural techniques.

The Creation of Sonara

The purpose of Sonara is defined in its statutes (1962): "to rationalize the commercialization of groundnuts within a framework of market regulations established by the government of Niger. To that end, it is authorized to conduct all commercial operations, including the purchase, storage, processing, packing, transport, maintenance, export, and sale of groundnuts." Sonara, a *société anonyme* (corporation) of mixed government and private ownership, began operations with capital of 120 million CFA francs. At the end of its first harvest, the capital was raised to 300 million CFA francs through the incorporation of reserves (see Table 3.2). Capital was divided into 12,000 shares having a nominal value of 25,000 CFA francs each.

Sonara holds a monopoly over export sales of groundnuts, inherited from the earlier, private export firms. Furthermore, the entire hierarchy of commerce was reexamined and the hegemony of the import-export houses was reduced: the *Alhazai* who had been simple buyers and the European commercial houses (their former patrons) became *organismes-stockeurs* (authorized warehousing organizations) when they agreed to participate in capitalizing the new company. From the time they were listed by Sonara at the beginning of each harvest "campaign," or season, these approved dealers received authorization to purchase an amount of groundnuts determined by the level of their activity during the preceding campaign. Such purchases were for the account of Sonara, which controlled their weekly expenditures and paid them commissions at a fixed rate established for each campaign (see Figure 3.3).

Table 3.2 Equity Capital in Sonara (in millions of CFA francs)

	Amount	Percentage
Government of Niger	20.0	6.5
Development Bank of Niger	62.5	21.0
Price Stabilization Board	62.5	21.0
Copro-Niger	5.0	1.5
Stockholders (private sector)	150.0	50.0
Total	300.0	100.0

Source: Sonara statutes

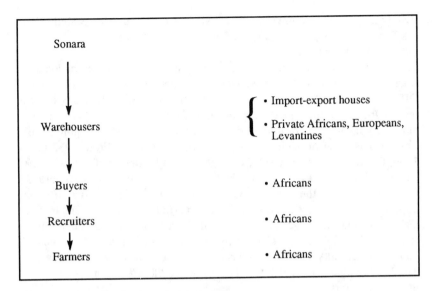

Figure 3.3 New Trade Hierarchy Under Sonara

Despite the new arrangements, many of the old regulations remained in effect: each year, announcements fixed the opening and closing dates of the trade and listed the official markets where buying operations were required to take place. Before each yearly season, the prices paid to producers were set by decree for each market. Finally, weighing-scale operators were required to be certified holders of an official permit provided by the local authorities.

The creation of Sonara profoundly changed the trading process. Its role was analogous to that of the Office de Commercialisation Agricole (OCA) created in Senegal shortly after that country's independence; OCA also held a monopoly over groundnut purchasing from cooperatives and from a reduced number of merchants. The OCA in turn sold to local processing plants or to exporting firms.

The Creation of Copro-Niger

Copro-Niger, a company engaged in both commerce and production, is a mixed-ownership enterprise. It was created to sell imported goods in competition with traditional commercial houses; to purchase foodstuffs such as millet, sorghum, and rice on local markets in order to distribute them for resale; and to buy small amounts of groundnuts in a limited number of markets. Its equity capital is 600 million CFA francs, the principal shareholders being the government of Niger and its Caisse de Stabilisation des Produits du Niger, in addition, Sonara, the UNCC, and several private individuals own shares.

In 1966, four years after its creation, Copro-Niger ceased to function as a stockpiler and later (1970) turned over its commercialization of cereals to the Office des Produits Vivriers du Niger (OPVN). From then on, it was responsible only for export of gum arabic, over which it still retains its monopoly, as well as for importation of current consumption requirements. Thus, it has gone through two stages since its creation: From 1962 until 1969, Copro-Niger simply sold, through its retail stores in all parts of the country (there were three in Maradi), the products it imported from abroad. From 1969 until the present, Copro-Niger has held a monopoly on importation of a number of essential products (milk concentrate, sugar, salt, tea, wheat flour, fabric, cigarettes, etc.). It abandoned retail sales in order to specialize in wholesaling, which consisted of advancing large quantities of goods to merchants for resale to consumers at prices fixed by Copro-Niger.[42] The 1969 reorganization of Copro-Niger favored the *Alhazai* and accelerated their economic rise.

To these long-term developments one must add a more recent one: in 1977 Copro-Niger reestablished retail shops, called *magazins temoins* (literally, "evidence stores"). Their purpose was to compete with private retail merchants and force them to respect government-imposed price controls.

The Organisation Commune Dahomey-Niger

In addition to the restructuring of the trade in groundnuts and imported manufactured goods, the government of Niger examined the transport problem, particularly the difficulties caused by Opération Hirondelle, which had been created and financially underwritten by the former metropole.

The governments of Niger and Dahomey decided to maintain the system and in 1959 approved the creation of the Organisation Commune Dahomey-Niger (OCDN, and, when Dahomey became Benin, OCBN), which was given responsibility for Opération Hirondelle and for running the Parakou-Cotonou railroad as well as the port of Cotonou. It encountered difficulties in 1963: following serious political problems between the two countries over border issues, OCDN's activities were suspended on December 27, 1963. However, they were restored relatively quickly (June 3, 1964), the differences between the two countries having been smoothed over.

All production from western Niger, from the *cercle* of Madaoua, and a portion of that from the *cercles* of Maradi and Zinder was exported via the Dahomean route. The Biafran war, which broke out in Nigeria in 1967, did not end until the defeat of the secession in 1970. Opportunities to export groundnuts through Lagos were much reduced, shifting a great deal of traffic to OCDN. This increased demand should have been good for OCDN. In fact, however, it was not, because not enough imported merchandise made the "upstream" trip; since many railroad cars returned to Niger empty, groundnut exporters found themselves paying a surcharge.[43]

Besides these effects, the Yaoundé convention required that groundnuts be marketed at world prices, which were markedly inferior to those guaranteed by France up until that time. Also, it was essential for Niger to keep down export freight costs.[44] This was impossible to do despite severe measures; for example, every year during Opération Hirondelle the government of Niger would prohibit imports transported through Nigeria.[45]

Currently, OCDN's activities have diminished because of the fall in groundnut production, and today the problem is reversed: vehicles arrive from the railhead at Parakou laden with the manufactured goods the country needs but usually return empty because of the lack of groundnuts or other export products (Figure 3.4).[46]

Creation of the UNCC

Created by Law 62-37 of September 20, 1962, the UNCC is a financially autonomous public enterprise. Its statutory purpose is "to develop mutual credit and cooperation among rural inhabitants in the Republic of Niger" and also "to support rural credit and cooperative associations in order to facilitate and coordinate their activities." The task of stimulating rural activity was, without a doubt, the most innovative aspect of this institution.

The system depended upon active cooperation within new institutions: the basic unit, the "active" village, was known as the groupement mutuel villageois (GMV). At the next higher echelon, the regroupement des villages animés (RVA) coordinated five to ten such villages that formed a single commercial market.[47]

Thus, for the marketing of groundnuts, the RVA was responsible for a storage plot and a weighing station to which the villagers could bring their groundnuts. Each plot was managed by a team of three or four persons chosen from among the producers. The team leader had the task of controlling purchases, overseeing stocks, and attracting buyers to the plot. However, the key person was the operator of the weighing scales, who received and processed incoming loads, which were recorded by a secretary. The smooth functioning of the market was assured by a market chief (*sarkin kasuwa*) elected by the team leaders. He controlled overall operations, had the scales tested, and verified payments to weighers. Assisted by a European bookkeeper, he checked the accounts of each plot every evening.

As a result of the installation of this cooperative system, the UNCC became more and more important; despite many administrative difficulties at the market level, the UNCC was the principal groundnut buyer in Niger from the 1964–1965 season on.

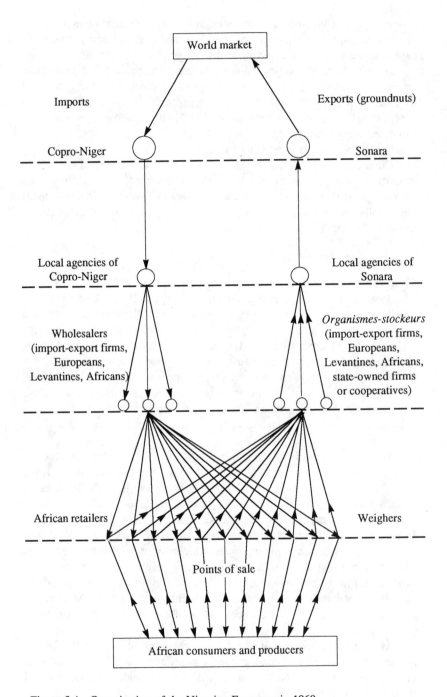

Figure 3.4   Organization of the Nigerien Economy in 1969

Evolution of Groundnut Markets Since 1962

The establishment of the institutions described above, beginning in 1962–1963, was accompanied by progress in production and in marketing of groundnuts, maintaining and even increasing the momentum of growth achieved during the preceding decade.

The Evolution of Production

Throughout Niger and especially in the region of Maradi, groundnut production made spectacular leaps during the years from 1960 until 1970 (see Figure 3.5). There were three essential reasons for this: except in 1968, rainfall was generally favorable toward agriculture and particularly toward groundnut farming; in 1971, however, precipitation began to diminish,

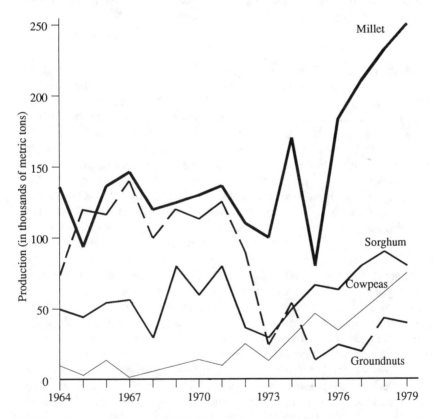

Figure 3.5   Production of Principal Food Grains, 1964–1979
Source: Grégoire and Raynaut, "Présentation générale du département de Maradi"

reaching a record low of only 287 millimeters in 1972.[48] Second, the growing weight of fiscal pressures, even after independence, obliged rural communities to increase the areas under groundnut cultivation in order to pay their taxes. The stagnation and even reduction in the price paid to groundnut producers during the period increased the problem (see Table 3.3); the farmers were constantly compelled to produce more. Third, the increases in production can be explained in some small measure by extension efforts: improved seeds, developed at the experimental station at Tarna, provided better results than local strains. Thereafter groundnut planting was no longer restricted solely to the well-watered, more fertile southern sections of the region but could be extended northward because the new varieties had shorter growing seasons. In addition, there were modest efforts to distribute fertilizer and better farm implements.

These diverse factors contributed to the spread of groundnut production in the *département* of Maradi, which rose from 71,000 metric tons (1964) to 136,000 metric tons (1967). This progress, coupled with the establishment of new marketing facilities, nevertheless created new problems.

Marketing Problems

Groundnut markets soared spectacularly in central Niger (*cercles* of Madaoua, Maradi, and Tessaoua): between 1962–1963 and 1967–1968, the amounts marketed rose from 30,631.54 to 86,561.35 metric tons. Also, in order to facilitate the movement of the crop, new trading posts were opened; at the time of the 1960–1961 harvest, there were a total of ten in the *département* of Maradi; by 1968–1969 there were twenty-six, of which sixteen were reserved exclusively for public, parastatal, and cooperative organizations, the others being for private dealers. These various changes all emphasize the great dynamism of the market, particularly that at Maradi (see Table 3.4).

The structural reforms undertaken beginning in 1962 created organizational problems for Sonara's "downstream" operations as well as for UNCC's on the "upstream" side. For Sonara, the principal problem concerned the acceleration of buying operations at the beginning of each trading season. Until 1960, as each season progressed the commercial houses managed the prices paid to farmers (guaranteed in any case since 1954) in order to achieve the tonnages needed to fulfill their contracts with European buyers. Beginning in 1962, the warehousers bought only to fill the quotas fixed for each of them by Sonara, which eliminated any possibility of buying additional amounts. Furthermore, the farmers could no longer hope for price increases after the season's end; short of cash (as always), they sold their entire crops at the beginning of the harvest. The delivery of massive amounts of groundnuts at the beginning of the season gave Sonara problems in financing (Sonara had to provide its buyers sizable advances), handling (shortages of bags interfered with storage operations), and transport (to the centers handling groundnut shelling and exports).

Table 3.3   Prices Paid by UNCC for Shelled Groundnuts (in CFA francs)

Years	Price per kilogram
1949/50	16.5
1950/51	14.5
1955/56	22.0
1956/57	21.0
1960/61	24.0
1964/65	21.0
1966/67	20.0
1968/69	18.0
1970/71	21.0
1971/72	23.0
1972/73	28.0
1974/75	45.0
1975/76	55.0
1977/78	69.0–78.0
1981/82	85.0
1982/83	100.0
1983/84	100.0

Table 3.4   Groundnut Tonnages Marketed at Maradi

Years	Tonnages
1962/63	5,409
1963/64	5,181
1964/65	5,336
1965/66	6,257
1966/67	8,332
1967/68	9,438
1968/69	4,012
1969/70	4,015
1970/71	3,661
1971/72	3,420
1972/73	3,026
1973/74	4,823
1974/75	796
1975/76	17

For UNCC, the problems were mainly administrative, notably in 1967–1968, when groundnut prices fell: the margin paid by Sonara diminished, while the official costs of marketing per metric ton of shelled nuts remained unchanged. Also, the many abuses that characterized the trade before 1962 reemerged. Losses and diversions were considerable. UNCC, like the commercial houses before it, unavoidably found itself dealing with unscrupulous or incompetent intermediaries. Its executives could only hope that, thanks to the creation of self-administered markets, the trade would be cleaned up and costs would be reduced.

The Marketing Agents

In addition to marketing problems, 1962 saw a change affecting the agents who took part in groundnut collections. When Sonara was created, the government of Niger encouraged the former exporters and traders to contribute capital to the new firm and become *organismes-stockeurs*. It also indicated a desire that Nigerien nationals become shareholders and play a role within the company. As a result, numerous Nigerien merchants, formerly simple buyers, found themselves on the same level as the European trading houses who also became dealers. (There were about twenty in 1964 in the region of Maradi.)

The initial equity capital of Sonara, fixed at 120 million CFA francs, was divided evenly between the public sector and the private sector (the *organismes-stockeurs*). The portion of business allotted to each private agent depended upon the tonnages the agent had handled, either as exporter or as trader, during preceding campaigns. Also, an estimated two-thirds of the private-sector shares (worth about 40 million CFA francs) were bought by former exporters or European, Lebanese, or Syrian traders. The Africans held the remainder, worth about 20 million CFA francs. Most of them, lacking the money to pay for their shares, obtained credit from the government's main financial arm, the Banque de Développement de la République du Niger (BDRN). Thus, *Alhaji* Ousmane, whose biography was presented above, eceived a loan from this bank in order to furnish the 2 or 3 million CFA francs that constituted his portion of Sonara's capital.

The dealers were chosen on the basis of the level of their earlier activity. All the Africans who had been traders for European firms and who had a certain commercial experience were permitted to buy in if they were interested (almost all of them were). The government of Niger intended to encourage the creation of a local commercial class and favored the presence within Sonara of as many Africans as possible, at least of those who had attained a certain economic credibility and a reputation for seriousness. Political criteria for choosing dealers did not appear to play a large part at the time, since the country had just recently become independent and political power was becoming established only gradually.

The dealers participated in the commercialization of groundnuts at a number of markets assigned to them before the opening of each season. The regulations required them to conduct their purchasing at specific markets and changed the roles of various commercial actors. This caused a sharp reduction in the activity of the European firms (Table 3.5).

One can see from Table 3.5 that the percentage share held by Levantines and Africans was unchanged during the period (whereas the tonnages they handled nearly doubled because of the very strong growth in production). The decline of the European firms benefited the state enterprises (Copro-Niger) or cooperatives (UNCC), which operated in "privileged" markets. In 1967–1968, UNCC was active in thirty-one of Niger's markets, while each private dealer operated in no more than two or three.

This growth of public and cooperative institutions intensified after 1968.[49] They were encouraged by the government of Niger's decree number 68/143 MAECI (Ministre des Affaires Economiques, Commerciales, et Industrielles) of October 29, 1968, Article 4 of which stated: "Participation of dealers in the purchasing of groundnuts from producers should be progressively replaced by that of public, parapublic, and cooperative institutions, in accordance with the government's program for developing agricultural cooperation." The authorities' objective, to diminish the participation of private dealers, applied particularly to foreigners. Article 2 of the decree stated further:

> In cases where purchasing locales formerly belonging to private dealers are transferred to the public, parapublic, or cooperative sector, the resulting potential reduction in purchases, expressed in a percentage of the previous year's program, will be imputed in thousandths to the quotas of non-Nigerien dealers. The thousandths thus available will be redistributed to Nigerien dealers pro rata according to the quotas to which they were entitled during the previous campaign.

In practice, this article hampered the large commercial firms more than the small European dealers, from whom the former often subcontracted portions of their quotas for a commission. The UNCC also had recourse to

Table 3.5   Participation of Agents in Groundnut Marketing (in percentages)

	1962/63 Season	1967/68 Season
European firms	41.7	26.0
Levantines or Africans	50.5	51.0
Public enterprises and cooperatives	7.8	23.0
	100.00	100.00

Source: Pehaut, L'arachide au Niger

this practice, which benefited a number of European and Levantine dealers. The latter in turn obtained quotas from the African dealers: the *Alhazai* sometimes had financial problems that prevented them from advancing enough money to achieve the quotas that Sonara had set aside for them. For fear of being penalized during the following season, they would appeal to more fortunate dealers to fill them.

The decree of October 29, 1968, most injured the activities of foreign dealers during a later period, the beginning of the 1970s, when the African dealers were suffering more and more from UNCC's competition. One of them recalled having abandoned the groundnut business "because the UNCC bought at practically every market in the bush and encouraged the farmers to sell it their harvests, and then because of the drought." Thus, the public sector expanded at the expense of the African private sector. This intense restructuring of commerce had its effects on Maradi.

Emergence of a City

In the course of the 1960s, Maradi saw a period of relative prosperity and important growth, which led in turn to a change in its governmental status: created in 1955, the mixed commune of Maradi became, as a result of the administrative reforms of July 17, 1964, an urban commune; in 1970 it became a *ville* (city), comparable to an *arrondissement*.

Its demographics during this period point up the change: the rate of growth, which had been 4.25 percent between 1950 and 1959, rose to 7.85 percent between 1959 and 1970. As for the population, it more than doubled, from 12,500 inhabitants in 1959 to 28,000 around 1970.

Along with Tessaoua, Maradi was the main trading point in the *département*. As Table 3.4 shows, the tonnages marketed increased and stimulated the creation of numerous jobs (market workers and vehicle loaders). At the same time, commerce had a "locomotive effect" on the whole urban economy, notably by attracting industry.

The Siconiger Vegetable Oil Mill

Even before World War II, there were many studies and experiments with vehicles to determine whether fuel could be made from oilseeds or fruits. Industry tried to develop motors operating on vegetable oils. These preoccupations led to creation of a small oil mill at Maradi in 1942 by the Société Algérienne des Pétroles Mory (SAPM), which was involved in shipping merchandise and fuels across the Sahara and elsewhere in West Africa generally.

At the beginning, the mill's production was very modest—five barrels of oil per day during the trading season, then a shutdown until the start of the next one. The output was for industrial use only, not for human consumption. Part of it was used by the Mory company and an associated firm, the Société Africaine des Transports, and part was sold to the French army base at Zinder.

The Mory firm later became the Société Africaine des Huiles (SAH), then Siconiger in 1954. It would have been difficult at that time, when groundnut production was growing enormously, to avoid increasing the mill's capacity. Mory, which was more interested in the transport business, decided to sell the mill to a group of industrialists from the north of France who were specialists in vegetable oils. A number of investment projects were completed and Siconiger established its own network of groundnut buyers who supplied the mill directly from the markets without working through the large commercial houses. The mill's production was reoriented toward cooking oils, most destined for export to metropolitan France.

By 1967–1968, Siconiger had a refining capacity of about 25,000 metric tons. Oil production, in keeping with that of groundnuts, grew from 900 metric tons in 1956–1957 to 7,309 in 1966–1967, and then to 13,000 during the 1971–1972 campaign.

Given the expansion of its activities, the oil mill needed a lot of employees, especially unskilled laborers. By 1967–1968, it had more than 100 permanent workers, and during the harvest season its staff swelled to about 250 people, who made the mill a very busy place.

The encouraging results obtained by Siconiger persuaded the management to increase refining capacity to 45,000 metric tons and to modernize the machinery (1974). The drought and the fall in groundnut production that followed made full use of this new oil production capacity impossible.

The Cotton Gin

Cotton is Niger's second leading agro-industry, but production on a vast scale did not get under way until after 1956 (there being no demand for it among local artisans), when the Compagnie Française de Développement des Textiles (CFDT) was given responsibility for its development.

Cotton requires favorable climatic conditions (rainfall of at least 500 millimeters per year) as well as appropriate soils (river valley clays). Production was concentrated almost entirely in the *département* of Tahoua, in the valley of the Ader Doutchi Maggia River, rather than in the *département* of Maradi, which is in the valley of the Maradi River. Nevertheless, the CFDT, which was a mixed-ownership company in which the French government held a majority of the shares, built a cotton gin at Maradi. Purchasing of raw cotton from producers was done by UNCC and the Projet de Développement Rural de Maradi; most of the ginned cotton was exported. The gin's operations expanded quickly, reaching capacity during the 1960s; capacity was increased in 1977. Like the groundnut oil mill, but on a much smaller scale, the cotton gin created employment. As in the case of groundnuts, drought disrupted the industry's progress.

The Construction Industry

With prosperity, demand for buildings and public works increased; this provided many projects for individuals as well as established firms. Table 3.6, which is based on statistics from the revenue service, indicates that the level of tax revenues on buildings multiplied threefold between 1960 and 1970.[50] In the course of that period, commercial buildings destined for trade in groundnuts as well as manufactured goods (distributed by Copro-Niger after 1969) were erected. By 1969, in that part of the Maradoua quarter situated behind the church, the first permanent villas were being built for rent to government officials or Europeans.

Beginning in 1968, the arrival of a new, energetic mayor allowed a number of improvement projects to be accomplished within the municipality: construction of paved roads and new trails to improve transportation; extension of running water pipes and installation of fire hydrants in new neighborhoods; electrification of the chief's area, the bus depot, and several main streets; construction of storm drains for the rainy season; and replacement of wooden stalls at the main market and the smaller market by modern, concrete stalls. All these accomplishments helped to revitalize and modernize the life of the city.

The Development of Urban Economic Activity

Changes in *patente* (business tax) levels, shown in Table 3.6, are only a very rough indicator of variations in general economic activity: the total amount of taxes collected grew from 15 million CFA francs in 1960 to just 18 million in 1971.[51] A detailed examination of the figures allows us to explain the changes.

When the revenue service was created in March 1959, it began a survey of economic activity that was completed in 1960, the base year for this analysis. For 1962, the strong decrease in business taxes is explained by the reorganization of the groundnut trade following the establishment of Sonara: traders and groundnut buyers were no longer subject to the business tax and instead paid taxes in the markets where they effected their transactions. For 1964, the data have an administrative, not an economic, explanation: following a change of incumbents in the chief inspector's position, the service was for a time without a leader; as a result, no final roll of business tax receipts could be established. In 1968, by contrast, one sees a very strong increase, no doubt because of the beginning of the Biafran war. Many Nigeriens and Nigerians transferred capital into the region in order to invest in commercial activities to supply northern Nigeria with various products that no longer arrived at Kano because of the war. In 1971, a large number of export licenses were issued, which explains the increase in business taxes: the war in Biafra having just ended, Nigeria began to import large quantities of meat and beans.

Table 3.6   Business Taxes and Real Property Taxes (in CFA francs)

Year	Business Tax Levels	Property Tax Levels
1959	8,564,418	1,208,684
1960	15,050,369	2,132,720
1961	13,095,538	2,252,160
1962	10,679,504	2,336,720
1963	12,180,858	2,334,650
1964	9,655,843	2,805,130
1965	10,503,913	4,495,674
1966	11,524,146	5,487,715
1967	10,788,826	5,594,368
1968	17,431,450	5,482,690
1969	13,931,875	5,995,550
1970	14,458,152	6,733,050
1971	18,124,674	8,323,517
1972	17,884,595	8,732,067
1973	20,059,574	9,384,500
1974	21,307,668	11,360,090
1975	35,289,120	14,492,654
1976	35,185,726	9,643,450
1977	30,804,240	10,776,809
1978	29,249,905	15,510,068
1979	30,515,656	13,818,508
1980	37,217,863	18,363,118
1981	39,591,743	18,681,418
1982	44,739,492	20,576,250
1983	74,216,617	40,451,463

Source: General Revenue Service, Maradi

Although these figures cover a long period, 1960–1971, they reflect only partially the reality of the economic transformations that the city experienced, and yet urban activities (crafts, small manufacturing, mini-commerce, services, etc.) undeniably proliferated. They profited from the effects of the groundnut trade, which increased the amount of money in circulation and improved the purchasing power of many inhabitants.

This evolution is, for example, quite clear with regard to transport of goods: in 1962, the statistics of the revenue service covered about thirty transport operators whose head offices were located at Maradi. The number exceeded fifty-four in 1966, eighty in 1972. Most of them were Nigeriens, who had gradually replaced the Europeans. The example of one of the large Maradi transport operators appears to represent one mode of wealth accumulation pursued by the *Alhazai*.[52]

Alhaji Boubakar began as an *apprenti-cale* for a European transport operator.[53] During his frequent travels he learned how to drive and how to do truck maintenance. As soon as he obtained a license, the European made him a driver, which he remained for several years. Having saved a bit of money, he bought one of his employer's trucks and began to work for himself. He obtained minor contracts in the area, mostly carrying groundnuts. One of his first jobs consisted of hauling groundnut shells into the bush from the shelling station at Tchadaoua. Bit by bit he paid off his loan and acquired a second truck with which he took part in Opération Hirondelle; later he worked for OCDN.

The intense trade in groundnuts during the 1960s helped him a great deal. By 1971, he had five or six trucks, a garage (bought from a Levantine), operating capital, and a hauling contract from the Siconiger oil mill. Since his capital was limited, an official of Siconiger helped him obtain a bank loan. This permitted him to undertake a major expansion of his business.

The drought, as well as the construction of the mining towns at Aïr, generated additional transport business for *Alhaji* Boubakar, who expanded his truck fleet. Currently he owns tractor-trailers for hauling merchandise, tank trucks, and heavy special-purpose vehicles used in public works construction, the latter to deliver paving materials to a European firm.

Alhaji Boubakar has diversified his business a little: other than transport, he has also invested in real estate, buying several villas. He has also extended his operations as far as Niamey and Kano and has correspondent arrangements at Parakou, Lagos, and Apapa.[54]

Conclusion

The policies adopted by the new leaders of Niger were designed to free the peasants from the constraints of the groundnut trade economy and mobilize them to take charge of their own development. The reorganization of the trade, which breached the hegemony formerly enjoyed by those symbols of colonial power, the commercial houses, was motivated by the same objectives that led to the cooperatives and the rural awakening movement. Such steps certainly had a psychological impact within Niger as well as abroad. For one thing, they removed control of the economy from agents installed by the former colonial power and transferred it to the government and indigenous nationals.

From the beginning, the government of Niger relied upon the existing commercial class to replace the European firms and other traders. For this reason, the various *Alhazai* selected by Sonara to become warehousers were given access to financing so they could become shareholders. Their operations prospered from 1962 until 1968, only to be hampered increasingly by competition from UNCC, which became very important because of its close ties with the government.

Did the political/bureaucratic class that grew larger and larger after independence enter into competition with the merchant class? The two groups first took over from the previous governmental and economic apparatus; after that, their interests diverged and they contended for control of resources produced by the groundnut sector, with the government attempting to gain control over the economy by creating new institutions. Probably the *Alhazai* profited relatively little from the new groundnut system, since they were very quickly forced out of the market by the UNCC; they would have made more money under the old system.

The new system was soon destabilized by the drought, whose onset was foreshadowed in 1968 and again in 1971. The drought profoundly changed agricultural conditions in the region of Maradi and, on a grand scale, all over the Sahel.

NOTES

1. Under the French colonial administration, a *cercle* was a political subdivision, roughly equivalent to a county, within a larger region—Translator.

2. The facts underscore the artificial character of this frontier.

3. Aboubakar Alio Yenikoye, "La justice du droit local." Government of Niger archival document.

4. S. Baier and P. E. Lovejoy, "The Desert Side Economy of the Central Sudan," *International Journal of African Historical Studies* 8, 4 (1975), pp. 551–581.

5. Baier, *An Economic History of Central Niger.*

6. Guy Nicolas, "Etudes des marchés en pays haoussa," *Documents ethnographiques*, Bordeaux, 1964.

7. The Tamanrasset fair, which occurs every January, is one of the oldest traditions of commerce between the Arab and black African worlds. Its level of activity is still important, and it attracts merchants from many countries (Algeria, Niger, Nigeria, Mali, Libya, etc.).

8. M. Abadie, *La colonie du Niger (Afrique Centrale)* (Paris: Société d'éditions géographiques, 1927).

9. David, "Maradi, l'ancien Etat et l'ancienne ville."

10. Y. Pehaut, *L'arachide au Niger.* Institut d'Etudes Politiques, Centre d'Etudes d'Afrique Noire. (Bordeaux: A. Pedone, 1970).

11. The colonial government occasionally resorted to arbitrary measures, such as compulsory planting (*gingilé*), in order to make people grow groundnuts; these amounted to forced labor.

12. Thus, the governor of Niger declared (in a letter to the *commandant de cercle* of Maradi, dated January 29, 1954),

> The cultivation of groundnuts has now reached a level that must not be surpassed; despite the attractive prices offered to farmers, an expansion to the detriment of food production would be dangerous. It is my desire that not a single hectare of land used to cultivate millet or other foodstuffs be converted by farmers for groundnut production, and I request that you urge your local chiefs to continue their efforts over the coming months to prevent that from happening. (Presidential Archives, Niamey.)

The quantity marketed that year in the *cercle* of Maradi reached almost 26,000 metric tons. A dozen years later (1966) it had tripled, reaching 75,000 metric tons. Data from Claude Raynaut, "Le cas de la région de Maradi," in J. Copans, ed., *Sécheresses et famines du Sahel* (Paris: Maspéro, 1975).

13. The peasants called their groundnut plantings "tax fields" (*gonan limpo*).

14. Raynaut, "Le cas de la région de Maradi."

15. Before World War II, purchases were often made in British currency. In the Maradi region, two kinds of money circulated freely, the French franc and the British pound sterling. In December 1945, the government created a "colonial franc" with a face value different from that of the French franc.

16. J. D. Collins, "The Clandestine Movement of Groundnuts Across the Niger-Nigeria Boundary," *Revue Canadienne des Etudes Africaines*, 10, 2 (1976), pp. 259–276.

17. Nicolas, "Etudes des marchés en pays haoussa."

18. The underlying legislation (enacted before World War II) contained no provisions regarding price fixing, which was not introduced until 1952; the decree of November 13, 1954, provided particulars.

19. The buyers were dependent upon the traders (or the exporters in cases where the firm did not resort to traders). For example, Elias Issa became a trader for CNF. *Alhaji* Daouda was a buyer before he became a trader himself for SCOA. In 1950 he bought shelled groundnuts for that firm and unshelled nuts for the oil mill belonging to Siconiger.

20. Nicolas, "Etudes des marchés en pays haoussa."

21. G. Mainet and Guy Nicolas, "La Vallée du *Goulbin* Maradi, enquête économique," *Documents des Etudes Nigériennes* (IFAN-CNRS, No. 16). The buyers responsible for weighing the harvest were called "sons of the balance-scale" (*dan balas*). The trader who was their patron (*uban-gida*) would provide them scales and bags and would advance them the funds needed to pay for the groundnuts. Accounts were settled during a meeting (*balas*) at which the trader brought together all of his buyers.

22. For a time, the government issued certificates to groundnut farmers good for the purchase of fabric in lieu of payment.

23. Before the establishment of Opération Hirondelle, the branches of commercial houses were supplied through Kano, where they had their regional headquarters.

24. *Alhaji* Maman dan Dano was also a municipal counsellor, giving him political importance at the local level.

25. Michel Agier, *Commerce et sociabilité: les négociants soudanais du quartier Zongo de Lomé (Togo)*, Collection Mémoires No. 99 (Paris: ORSTOM, 1983).

26. In Hausa, the word *maigoro* means "he who has colas."

27. According to one informant, *Alhaji* Gambo Maigoro also developed links with merchants at Mzab.

28. The cola business is also frequently conducted on credit, which permits some dealers to set up formal service relationships with retailers.

29. He was a distributor for silver coins bearing the effigy of Maria Theresa, empress of Austria, imported by the Banque d'Afrique de l'Ouest; African women used the coins as jewelry.

30. We shall see that at the death of a merchant, the commercial enterprise is divided among the heirs and that there exists no continuity nor any great commercial "dynasties" such as those in Europe at the time of the Renaissance, for example.

31. Sonara, the state-controlled groundnut marketing company, is more fully described in the text.—Translator.

32. The principal African merchants in and around Maradi started as buyers for Elias Issa, then became agents for the commercial firms, among whom competition was so fierce that they made every effort to recruit the Africans who controlled the best commercial networks.

33. Guy Nicolas, "La pratique traditionelle du crédit au sein d'une société sub-saharienne (Vallée de Maradi, Niger)," in *Cultures et développement* (Louvain: Catholic University, 1974), pp. 737–773.

34. Cf. Pehaut, *L'arachide au Niger.*

35. This would be one of the principal reasons for the failure of Elias Issa, who could never recover all the money he loaned to his buyers.

36. African merchants rarely handled both types of commerce systematically; rather, they specialized in either one or the other.

37. This limited success depended for most upon the links they had been able to establish with the firms. The latter preferred to deal with a few individuals in whose ability and seriousness they had confidence.

38. Since he is still active in business, his identity is camouflaged here.

39. According to a European who has lived many years in Maradi, "As soon as an African acquires any money, he goes into the transport business." At that time the purchase of a truck represented not only a symbol of success, but also an important element employed by some merchants in the process of capital accumulation.

40. An *organisme-stockeur* was a merchant officially authorized to warehouse groundnut inventories during the interval between purchase from farmers and sale to Sonara. The activity is further discussed in the text—Translator.

41. We shall see below that it is acquired outside the framework of familial relationships.

42. In order to be certified by the company, merchants were required to be listed in the local roster of businesspeople, to pay a *patente*, or special tax, and to prove their Nigerien citizenship; foreigners were allowed to participate if they were holders of a special authorization to do business in Niger.

43. Pehaut, *L'arachide au Niger.*

44. OCDN was experiencing severe operating deficits. [The Yaoundé Convention, ratified in June 1964, was the first trade and economic aid agreement between the members of the European Community and the newly independent developing nations. It has been superseded by a series of agreements known as the Lomé Convention—Translator.]

45. Article 52 of decree number 60-214 MAECI, November 7, 1960, stipulated that "in order to assure the minimum return freight needed during the eighth Opération Hirondelle, as of November 1, 1960, and continuing until the end of the harvest, the minister of economic affairs will reject any application for foreign exchange for transport costs via Nigeria of merchandise destined for the region of Maradi (*cercles* of Konni, Madaoua, Maradi and Tessaoua)."

46. In 1969 Copro-Niger had a monopoly on imports of several products classed as necessities: sugar, green tea, cloth, wheat flour, matches, cigarettes, sweetened condensed milk, and sea salt. Note that for those items over which Copro-Niger has no monopoly, the diagram is identical to that in Figure 3.5. Now, however, all wholesalers in Niger may import such merchandise: the foreign import-export houses have lost their monopolies.

47. Cf. Pehaut, *L'arachide au Niger.*

48. Average annual rainfall for the period 1946–1965 was about 650

millimeters at Maradi. Cf. J. Koechlin, "Rapport d'étude sur le milieu natural et les systèmes de production," University of Bordeaux II, 1980.

49. The PPN/RDA political party in power at the time had branches in even the most remote reaches of the bush. It intervened in numerous ways in village life, especially favoring the activities of public institutions.

50. The tax rate for developed property is based upon annual rental value actually realized, or which could be realized, by its owner. An abatement for maintenance is applied (40 percent for dwellings, 50 percent for industrial and commercial buildings). The tax rate on the net rental value is on the order of 20 percent.

51. Every individual in Niger who engages in commerce, industry, or a profession not included on a limited list of exceptions, is required to pay the *patente* tax.

52. Since he is still in business, his true identity has not been revealed in the discussion.

53. An *apprenti-cale* (literally, "wedge-apprentice") is a boy or young man who accompanies his employer on trips; whenever his employer is absent, he watches the vehicle and puts chocks under the wheels to keep it from rolling.

54. His activities are now equally divided between Niger and Nigeria.

Photo 1 Commercial buildings

Photo 2 Cola nut vendors

Photo 3 Unloading a truck from Lomé at a Nitra warehouse

Photo 4 Nigerian trucks loaded with goods in transit through Niger

Photo 5 Foreign-currency traders set up for business near the bank

Photo 6 CFDT cotton gin

Photo 7   Highway service station, Maradi
(selling gasoline smuggled from Nigeria)

Photo 8 Youth working at
a metal furniture factory

Photo 9 Cart manufacturing workshop

Photo 10 Mosque built by a rich *alhaji*

4

Dynamism and Diversity: From Regional to Global Trade

EFFECTS OF DROUGHT ON TRADE
IN AGRICULTURAL AND PASTORAL PRODUCTS

The Sahel is a place where famines are given proper names, like hurricanes, to serve as historical markers. Drought is a constant menace. The disaster at the beginning of the 1970s was unforeseen but inevitable, given that good years are eventually followed by bad, with all the damage that bad years inflict upon farm and pasture.

The drought of the 1970s can be explained as a series of disturbances to the pattern of rainfall, as disjunctions in the amount of water distributed across time and space. It may even have been a result of various disequilibria that became accentuated during the colonial period and the early years of independence.

Certainly, the drought caused profound changes in the production and marketing of farm products. Its most striking effect was the net loss to groundnut culture, abandoned by rural communities compelled to grow food as their highest priority.[1] Food production was further stimulated by demand from cities, whose burgeoning populations required dependable sources of supply.

The drought also wrought its ills on livestock herders, who figured among its principal victims as they watched their herds decimated. Speculators in the towns, by contrast, realized enormous profits from exports to Nigeria of livestock and meat, hastily brought to market to avoid loss by starvation and thirst.

The Decline of Groundnut Agriculture

The development of groundnut production for commercial purposes was very intense during the 1960s. The drought initiated a brutal drop in production levels, disrupting markets and creating severe problems for Sonara and its private dealers.

The Collapse of Production

During the period 1971–1975, rainfall recorded at Maradi and all over Niger was far below average. In addition, food production was insufficient to meet the population's needs. As a result, groundnut production fell: from 136,000 metric tons in 1967, it declined to 15,000 in 1975, climbing to 38,000 in 1980 (see Figure 3.5). There are several explanations for the variations:[2]

- The dry years forced farmers to give priority to food production in order to feed their families. This need produced a decline in groundnut plantings, which had been increased originally at the expense of millet; this had left the rural community particularly vulnerable to climatic hazards.
- The goad of fiscal necessity, which had been one of the motivations for introducing and then expanding groundnut farming, diminished; by 1977 it had been almost completely eliminated. The government of Niger abolished the tax on livestock and the minimum personal tax, lightening the need for cash among heads of households and thus bringing great relief to peasant communities, for whom taxes had been very onerous (only a minor *arrondissement* tax was imposed as of 1986).
- Since the drought, food production had become the focus of intense commercialization and was likely to become, at least in part, a cash crop, which formerly had been true only of groundnuts. The cash market for food crops, which had stimulated the increase in cereals production, resulted from the need to supply the urban centers.
- Plantings of a new, drought-resistant, short-cycle variety of cowpeas occupied more and more land, replacing some groundnuts.[3] Intense demand in Nigeria, where the prices were very attractive, made cowpeas a high-revenue cash crop.
- In the early 1980s, attacks from parasites as well as difficulty in obtaining high-quality seeds slowed resumption of groundnut production.

Taken together, these diverse factors have contributed to the decline of groundnut agriculture. However, interviews with farmers do not reveal any deep-seated rejection of groundnuts. Prices, which were only 21 CFA francs per kilogram in 1971, quintupled after stagnating for many years, becoming very interesting (100 CFA francs per kilogram of shelled nuts during the

1982–1983 campaign). Yet, it is neither desirable nor probable that production and marketing will regain the levels of the 1960s, because the world market for vegetable oils is no longer favorable to groundnuts because of strong competition from sunflower seeds, soybeans, and other oilseeds.

Marketing Problems

The decline in groundnut production has naturally affected the market, disturbing the operations of Sonara and its private dealers.

Sonara. Having marketed 70,725 metric tons during the 1967–1968 campaign, Sonara handled only 780 metric tons in 1975–1976 and 24,000 in 1980–1981. Despite this weak performance, the organizational structure described above remained unchanged. In order to keep Sonara in operation, however, in 1975 the government of Niger assigned it a monopoly over marketing and export of cowpeas (*niébé* in French, *wake* in Hausa).[4] Production of cowpeas has increased spectacularly in recent years, especially in the north and east of the *département*, where they have replaced groundnuts (see Figure 4.1). The success is due to distribution of a new variety (TN 8863, called *Dan Cana*) now in commercial use and beginning to be exported to Nigeria. Marketing is organized in a manner identical to that of groundnuts (using the same network of private dealers), and all transactions outside of official channels are forbidden. However, official marketing represents only a small proportion of total production.[5]

The very small quantities marketed in 1980–1981 (see Table 4.1) are due to price differentials: the official market price is 45 CFA francs per kilogram, while on the parallel market it is 75 CFA francs and in the market at Sabon Birni, just across the border in Nigeria, it is 120 to 130 CFA francs per kilogram. These gaps explain why the vast majority of sales are fraudulent. The dealers, several of whom act as agents for very wealthy *Alhazai* in Maradi or Nigeria, buy before (or sometimes well after) the official market hours. Most of the farmers go to them to sell the better part of their harvest.[6]

These activities raise questions about Sonara's operations, which should be very successful given its official monopoly on cowpeas. The dealers remain in business because they stay close to the farmers, giving them more advantageous terms than any the state enterprises offer. The state's monopoly, moreover, is easily evaded: the energetic merchants easily outmaneuver the state's administrative inertia, whether in buying up harvests at the farm gate or selling goods in the bush. Lacking flexibility, the state works at cross-purposes with local business customs, which limits its effectiveness.

The organismes-stockeurs. The groundnut shortage provoked the final retreat of the European commercial houses, which closed their trading posts in order to concentrate solely on import-export and wholesale distribution.

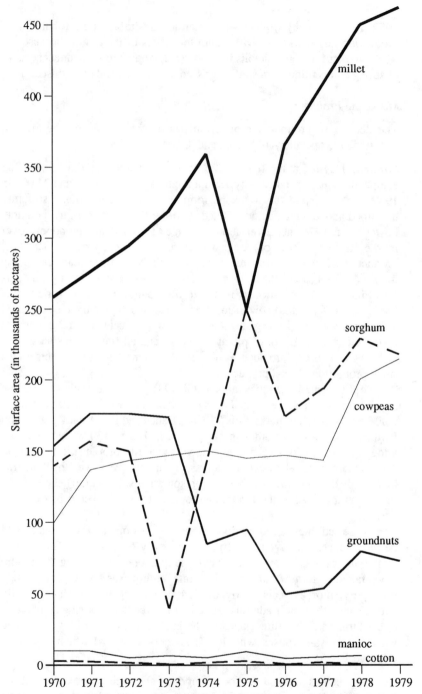

Figure 4.1   Variation in Areas Cultivated for the Principal Crops, 1970–1979
Source: Grégoire and Raynaut, "Présentation générale du département de Maradi"

Table 4.1 Marketing of Cowpeas by Sonara

Campaign	Tonnage Marketed	Percentage of Production
1978/79	11,252.3	19.5
1979/80	28,765.0	47.6
1980/81	2,588.4	3.7

They were followed by the European merchants and the Levantines, to such an extent that Sonara now has only African dealers. The latter, while remaining official shareholders in the company, rarely participate any longer in the groundnut harvest because of strong competition from UNCC.[7] In recent years the Projet de Développement Rural de Maradi has procured most of whatever minimal tonnages have been available.

In addition, some of the dealers, heavily indebted to Sonara and unable to recoup the advances they paid to farmers, were unable to deliver the amounts they promised. For example, *Alhaji* Ousmane collected only 20 metric tons of groundnuts in 1980–1981, although in better times he had handled from 2,000 to 3,000 metric tons.

Those few *Alhazai* whose fortunes peaked during the 1960s thanks to the groundnut trade have lost their influence and their prestige. They no longer count among the most powerful *Alhazai* in Maradi because their ability to invest was often too limited to allow them to put their capital into other activities and therefore to "bet on many tables."[8] As a result, they were very vulnerable hostages to the groundnut business. When the drought arrived, many of them went into the trade, and a few even into the production, of foodstuffs. Others abandoned the agricultural sector, going into some other line entirely. *Alhaji* Nabangui, who had been a groundnut buyer for CNF and later a warehouser for Sonara, became a "specialist" in buying merchandise seized by the customs service, which he resold at a nice profit.

The Development of Food Production and Marketing

Beyond any doubt, the drought was the catalyst for this particular change.

How Agricultural Production Changed

Under the traditional agrarian system, millet was a commercial crop, which the farmers traded with the Tuareg for crystalline salt brought down from the Saharan oases, Bilma and Fachi, and for the cowrie shells needed to pay annual tribute. The region thus fed a part of the Sahara.

Groundnut agriculture was introduced and expanded at the expense of at least some millet and sorghum production, and (as some officials had feared) in time it severely compromised the food security of rural communities. From then on, any drop in production was liable to manifest itself as a grave subsistence problem. This phenomenon began to appear at the beginning of the 1960s. During that decade climatic conditions were generally favorable for agriculture; for example, in 1964 total national production provided 290 kilograms of cereals per person, a figure exceeded in the *département* of Maradi. (The basic requirement for one person is generally estimated to be about 250 kilograms of cereals a year.) In the following years the situation began to deteriorate, and in 1973 there was an important cereals deficit (about 150 kilograms per person), bringing on a famine that lasted until 1975 (when the deficit was 170 kilograms per person).

Since 1973, the area cultivated in millet and sorghum has grown (see Figure 4.1), permitting gains in production (Figure 3.5). This has ameliorated the situation; in fact, the rural development ministry's statistics show a surplus for 1976–1979, with 320 kilograms per person for 1979. Even though the official figures have to be used cautiously, it appears that an equilibrium in foodstuffs can be attained nationally whenever climatic conditions are favorable. This is not to deny that the real food supply for the majority of the rural population remains precarious. Any bad climatic episode that hits the region hard risks unleashing new shortages.[9]

The farmers' steps to increase production were not intended solely to assure their future needs would be met nor to reconstitute depleted food stocks. The market value of millet and sorghum, which had not varied significantly for twenty years, also played a role.[10] These two cereals have become the subject of active trade, usually involving sales to the towns, which now allows farmers to obtain the money they need to satisfy various material needs and social obligations. In that sense, cereals have been substituted for groundnuts.

Cereals Marketing

The two main cereals marketing agencies are OPVN and the private merchants.[11] At least since the drought, the latter have perceived opportunities for high-stakes speculative gains in this important market. During the past few years this has generated tensions between the government of Niger, which is careful to regulate speculation in essential foodstuffs, and the *Alhazai*, some of whom are no longer content to be simple intermediaries between farmers and consumers but have also become millet growers themselves.

Supplying food to the town. Using a rationale similar to that which prompted creation of Sonara and Copro-Niger soon after independence, the government of Niger also intervened to regulate the cereals markets, creating the OPVN in 1970. According to its statutes, this entity is intended to achieve the following purposes:

- Organize food markets and support food production;
- Make annual forecasts of resources and national food needs
- Plan and execute a program of storage, importation, and exportation for each commodity;
- Establish buffer stocks in order to stabilize producer and consumer prices;
- Take all useful measures to organize and control the procurement and sale of food products;
- Prepare to execute food aid programs based on national or international resources.[12]

This state institution played only a secondary role until 1981, and, as an examination of recent harvests clearly shows, it began to stabilize food prices only in 1982.

The 1980–1981 harvest. The role played by OPVN was quite modest in 1980–1981, since it handled only 15 percent of the cereals marketed in the town of Maradi. Most of what it obtained went to civil servants and employees of state enterprises (local offices, banks, etc.). Food was handed out according to lists of recipients at five distribution centers in various neighborhoods. Supplies depended upon whatever was on hand—on the average, about 1 metric ton of cereals per neighborhood per day.

The OPVN encountered many difficulties in procuring food, even though since 1978 it had held a monopoly (in theory, at least) on purchases throughout the official campaign period (September to March). In practice, the *Alhazai* paid no attention to the prohibitions and conducted business as usual during the campaign. They also bought millet through the intermediary of their marketing networks, which extended to the remotest parts of the bush. They offered prices to producers that were well above those paid by OPVN (8,000 CFA francs per 100-kilogram bag instead of 5,000 CFA francs). It was easy to move grain out of the villages once the official season ended, thus avoiding seizure. Purchases were also made in the course of the growing period by buying crops standing in the fields, the farmer thus selling a portion of his future harvest. Alternatively, the merchant could buy at the end of the growing season, speculating on the opening date of the impending official buying campaign, during which OPVN had a monopoly. The amounts of millet offered then were significant because the farmers needed additional money to meet various expenses (marriages and religious festivals). Thus, the prices paid to producers then were lower than those that applied later in the campaign.[13]

The millet sold under such conditions was harvested during March and sold in the town markets, where prices always increase as the end of the dry season approaches. Such speculation was very profitable in 1980–1981 (see Table 4.2), especially because of poor harvests in the *départements* of Niamey and Tahoua, which needed outside supplies.

Table 4.2   Free Market Prices for Millet at Maradi (in CFA francs per 100-kilogram bag)

Year	September	January–February	May
1977/78	4,000	7,000	7,400
1978/79	—	—	—
1979/80	5,000	6,000	9,000
1980/81	8,000	—	25,000
1981/82	9,000	14,000	8,000
1982/83	10,000	9,000	9,000
1983/84	—	9,000	11,000

The 1981-1982 harvest. In May 1981 the government attempted to make the *Alhazai* aware of the problems caused by the rampant speculation. At meetings held at the prefecture in Maradi, officials asked them to help bring down prices. When the effort failed, the government tried to seize millet in the markets in order to resell it to consumers at OPVN prices. The merchants boycotted the markets, and, fearing shortages, the authorities backed down.

The government wanted to avoid seeing millet prices reach very high levels again at the end of the dry season (a 100-kilogram bag had cost 25,000 CFA francs in May 1981 as opposed to 9,000 CFA francs the preceding year). It restored OPVN's original role, which was to sell food to the entire population, not just to civil servants, and took steps to assure that OPVN would be able to sell large amounts of millet from the beginning of April, the time of year when free market prices hit their maximum. It organized procurement efforts by raising the producer price (see Table 4.3) and by starting to buy as quickly as possible after the crops were harvested.

This gave the merchants only a few days to trade between the harvest's end and the imposition of OPVN's buying monopoly. As an additional measure, OPVN appealed to the traditional chiefs to impose a cereals quota on every village in the *département*. The purpose of this measure was to short-circuit the merchants at the village level, where they had many agents. The farmers, who had not had a good harvest in 1981, managed to deliver the required quotas, but OPVN still did not obtain the tonnages that it had targeted at the beginning of the campaign. It was forced to appeal to the *Alhazai* to import foreign cereals (US sorghum, Pakistani rice) in order to meet its requirements.

Beginning in April 1982, the millet bought by OPVN was sold to people in the urban centers, to herders, and to people in high-deficit rural areas. From then on, speculation diminished; OPVN had successfully reined in the merchants and stabilized grain prices. State intervention in the cereals markets had become imperative in order to control speculation and to pacify

Table 4.3   OPVN Buying and Selling Prices for Millet (in CFA francs per 100-kilogram bag)

Year	Producer Buying Price	Consumer Selling Price
1974/75	2,500	3,150
1975/76	2,500	3,150
1976/77	2,500	3,150
1977/78	3,500	5,000
1978/79	3,500	5,000
1979/80	4,000	5,000–6,000
1980/81	4,000–5,000	7,000
1981/82	7,000	10,000
1982/83	8,000	12,000
1983/84	8,000	12,000

Source: OPVN

discontented citizens, who had lost purchasing power as a result of millet prices (this included Peul and Tuareg herders as well as those farmers who had to buy because their own supplies were exhausted). Nevertheless, it was done at the expense of farmers in general, who were forced to sell to OPVN at prices below those offered earlier by the merchants.

The 1982–1983 harvest. The rainy season of 1982 having yielded good harvests in Niger, OPVN abandoned quotas at the village level in favor of a single, national target. Marketing was aimed at the cooperatives, leaving the chiefdoms responsible only for propagandizing the farmers.

The financial means of the office were reinforced in order to avoid expensive imports. This measure, combined with the good harvest, produced strong marketing results (37,222 metric tons versus 7,788 the previous year) by January. The merchants then bought the remaining surplus in the villages. The year's abundance of millet caused a brutal fall in market prices: OPVN sold at 12,000 CFA francs per 100-kilogram bag whereas the merchants offered it at about 9,000 CFA francs.[14] As a result, consumers turned to the free market, leaving OPVN with considerable unsold surpluses (some 30,000 metric tons as of September 1983). The market was obeying its own laws, demonstrating again that state enterprises such as OPVN and Sonara lacked flexibility in their operations, while the Alhazai quickly adapted to changing market conditions, even though their fast actions sometimes skirted the law.

The 1983–1984 harvest. The following year, OPVN cut back its buying operations in order to sell down its existing stockpiles. The number of buying points in the bush was reduced to keep farmers from selling their surpluses to OPVN. In addition, the farmers found themselves selling to merchants, but at prices less attractive than those paid by OPVN (4,500 to 5,000 CFA francs compared with 8,000). Given the large surplus OPVN held, there was no room for speculation; in May 1984, the price of millet on the free market was still lower than that at OPVN. Moreover, it is probable that the government of Niger has been able to stabilize grain prices during the ensuing three years and thereby eliminate speculation by the *Alhazai*.

The conflict pitting the *Alhazai* against the Nigerien state reveals the divergence of their interests. The *Alhazai* are guided by profit; the state, which is to say, the political elite, is anxious to avoid popular discontent that might threaten stability. Today's political leaders remember that the government's lax attitude toward the merchants' enriching themselves during the drought (often with the complicity of civil servants) was one of the reasons for the fall of President Diori Hamani's regime.

The role of self-sustenance. Some officials estimate that 25 to 35 percent of Maradi's food needs are met by city dwellers growing their own crops. The 1982 census indicates that farmers represent almost 15 percent of the town's heads of household. This figure varies from one neighborhood to another, being higher in the old ones (Bagalam, 34 percent; Limantche, 28 percent; Yan Daka, 25 percent) than the new (Sabon Carré, 7 percent; Soura Boulde, 6 percent), and higher among old settlers than among people more recently arrived in town.

To these "pure" cultivators must be added quite a number of family heads who, although not farmers themselves, receive some income from agriculture. Many send money to relatives in the villages who hire labor to work their fields. The harvests are then brought to town, where they add substantially to the budgets of many citizens.

Therefore, self-sustenance is fairly important; regardless of the social status of individuals, according to one informant, "everyone does a little farming in the rainy season." He adds, not without a trace of malice, "Lots of civil servants are self-sufficient in food."[15]

Large-scale farming by city dwellers. Since agriculture has begun to produce economic rents, with grain production especially rewarding, some *Alhazai* are no longer content to be intermediaries; they have become producers as well. This reversal of the earlier situation results in large part from the drought.

As Raynaut has reported, prior to 1974 certain *Alhazai* already owned farmland, but they "pursued economic returns much less than the projection of an image of wealth—that of a powerful man whose granaries overflow with inexhaustible reserves and who can, in case of need, provide succor to those who have placed themselves under his protection." His data indicate that such operations cost more than they produce for their proprietors.[16]

According to recent estimates, agriculture has now become profitable. Some *Alhazai* who had been groundnut buyers (see the biographic sketch of *Alhaji* Ousmane in Chapter 3) have switched to grain production, much as many farmers did. They make use of their extensive real estate holdings (tens and even hundreds of hectares) at the edge of town. They turn the land over to managers who farm it with mechanical equipment and day labor recruited in the villages. The harvest is stored for several months and then sold at high prices during the dry season. In 1980, one merchant in Maradi harvested 500 metric tons of millet from a plot he owns in the bush. Sold toward the end of the dry season at free market prices, it produced revenue of about 45 million CFA francs. Even after subtraction of labor and transport costs, the profit was substantial.

Other than these major efforts, townspeople (merchants and civil servants alike) exercise stronger and stronger control over the land near Maradi, in parts of the Maradi River valley where irrigated farming is feasible. The fruits and vegetables cultivated on plots constitute a considerable revenue.[17]

Since the drought, speculation has turned more and more toward agriculture, despite the risks presented by the vagaries of the climate. This is not limited to Maradi—it is happening all over the Sahel.[18]

The Livestock Markets

Although the drought severely damaged the livelihood of sedentary farm communities, it was perhaps even more injurious to the nomadic population. The migrations of Peul, Bouzou, and Tuareg tribes toward the southern parts of the Sahel and into urban centers began as early as 1970, reaching its maximum intensity between October 1973 and May 1974.[19] For four years their herds had suffered, many animals dying from thirst. The surviving livestock, reduced to skeletons, was sold in the markets at derisory prices that enabled speculators to reap enormous profits.

Changes in Herd Size

Figure 4.2 traces herd size from 1968 to 1978. The year 1968 was chosen as a reference point because it reflects the situation before the drought began. The cattle herds actually began to diminish following the dry season in 1968–1969. They were recovering until 1972, but the drought of 1972–1973 caused a brutally rapid fall in the number of animals, from 510,000 head (1972) to 356,000 (1973), decimating the local herd. Since then, the numbers have increased and the herd has been reconstituted.[20] As for small ruminants, the figures are quite similar, except recovery was much quicker and the number of sheep and goats is now greater than it was in 1968. The camel herd has also recovered to its previous size.

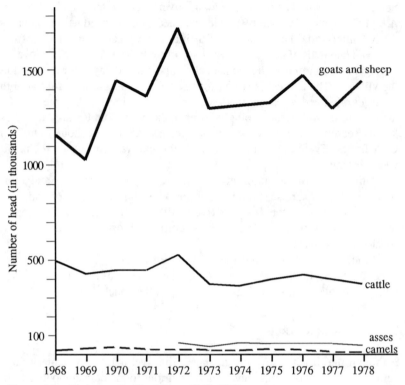

Figure 4.2   Variations in Herd Size, 1968–1978
Source: Livestock Service, *Département* of Maradi

Changes in Prices for Animals

Trade in livestock, always important in the region of Maradi, has traditionally been oriented toward Nigeria, which consumes large amounts of meat. Ever since the beginning of the Biafran war disrupted markets in Nigeria, exports to that country have increased. Because it considers meat exports beneficial, the government of Niger has authorized many of its citizens—particularly *Alhazai*—to take part in the trade, which continued after the war ended. The drought interfered with the trade, but it permitted certain traders to engage in very profitable speculations at the expense of the nomads.

In 1974 the Peul, Bouzou, and Tuareg herders, having lost a great many animals, tried to sell a portion of those remaining in order to salvage at least something. The *Alhazai* took advantage of the situation by proposing contemptuous prices, forcing the owners to "dump" their livestock: in a normal year a full-grown steer would have sold for about 20,000 CFA francs, a goat for 2,000 to 2,500 CFA francs, and a ram for 3,000 to 3,500 CFA francs; Table 4.4 shows 1974 prices at the market in Maradi.

Some of the beneficiaries of these unfair sales slaughtered their animals and sold the products as smoked meat in Nigeria, where they were officially prohibited. Others, by contrast, intended to keep their animals alive for two or three years, hoping to sell them at much better prices. The latter effort involved considerable risk, as many animals were beyond recovery. However, speculation enriched quite a few butchers, merchants, truckers, and even civil servants.[21] They profited from the devastation of the nomads' livelihood.[22]

Reductions of herd size in 1973 and 1974 were followed by sharp price inflation (Figure 4.3). In 1978, adult cattle and sheep cost six times the 1968 prices, while pack camels and three-year-old goats had tripled in price. The inflation was stimulated by Nigerian merchants who came to buy animals in Niger for export on the hoof, often illegally. Such trade was then the main commercial activity in the busy market at Djibya, on the southern side of the border. There, animals are bought and transported by truck to the slaughterhouses at Kano, Kaduna, and even Lagos. A great many *Alhazai* are involved to one degree or another in this trade, and many of them own livestock as a sideline to their main activities.[23]

Table 4.4 Examples of Livestock Prices During the Drought (in CFA francs)

Example	Quantities Sold	Price
1	10 cattle + 5 sheep	45,000
2	20 cattle + 10 goats	75,000
3	1 steer + 5 sheep	17,000
4	1 steer + 2 ewes + 3 goats	3,000
5	6 goats	4,000

Conclusion

At the beginning of the 1970s, when groundnut agriculture suddenly collapsed, Maradi might have slowly fallen into lethargy—as did, for example, the town of Louga in Senegal, whose early growth was similar to Maradi's.[24] That did not happen, and Maradi was able to continue growing, thanks to a diversification of its activities. The town's commercial dynamism strongly contrasts with the stagnation then occurring in agriculture. For the analysis of the formation of a merchant bourgeoisie, the principal subject of

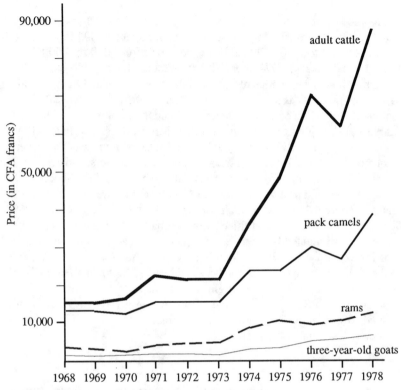

Figure 4.3   Variations in Livestock Prices, 1968–1978
Source: Grégoire and Raynaut, "Présentation générale du département de Maradi"

this study, the drought certainly was a pivotal period. It dealt a fatal blow to those *Alhazai* whose operations were solely oriented toward groundnuts, who found themselves destitute as a result of failing to diversify. For others, on the contrary, it brought benefits, allowing them to realize high profits either from the sale of livestock, trade in grain, or the transport and distribution of foreign food aid to impoverished areas. The drought is incontestably the source of some *Alhazai* fortunes.

In recent years the speculators have moved beyond trade in agropastoral products to their actual production. Over the long run, this dynamic might lead to a class of rich landed proprietors and a dispossessed rural proletariat. However, the flow of investment remains too timid for such a situation to develop any time soon. Still, the figures suggest that a transformation is in progress: it is not by accident that in 1984 the richest of Maradi's *Alhazai*, a millet farmer among other occupations, was elected president of the *département*'s cooperative members within the government's newly formed

Société de Développement.[25] In that capacity he will represent the farmers in the new legislature and will certainly profit from the position.

Finally, the vital equilibrium of rural communities remains permanently precarious because of the threat of drought: any new climatic accident comparable to that of 1974 would bring about a new famine and an acceleration of the exodus. The flow of migrants occurred because agriculture was not able to provide enough resources. This is usually temporary and has little effect on agricultural activities, but sometimes it is transformed into permanent displacement to the towns; the demographic dynamics of Maradi certainly show a sharp increase during the past ten years.

The political and economic choices that will be taken concerning development will have a decisive influence on rural communities. Perhaps, under pressure from organizations such as the World Bank, the decisions taken will favor small agricultural entrepreneurs, those of means financially and technically, at the expense of support to the whole rural community. That will accelerate the arrival in town of many more rural dwellers, people whose sole resource will be the sale of their physical labor.

THE GROWTH OF LARGE-SCALE COMMERCE

While trade in agricultural products was profoundly reoriented by the creation of state enterprises, trade in manufactures was similarly transformed by the reorganization of Copro-Niger, which enabled a few *Alhazai* to strengthen their commercial positions.

Copro-Niger aside, however, the central factor of the period 1970 to 1983 was the growth of trade with Nigeria. The increase began in 1967, the year of the Biafran secession, which disrupted Nigeria's internal trade by cutting off the north from its traditional sources, the ports on the southern coast. Maradi became one of the main towns supplying northern Nigeria with bales of frippery (secondhand clothing), cloth, cigarettes, and other items, and it remained a transit point when the war ended in 1970. Success in the import-export business enabled the *Alhazai* to make huge sums of money, which they invested in a variety of activities on both sides of the border. Maradi and the *Alhazai* owe their prosperity to these activities, which continue to this day.

It must be emphasized that while the decade following independence was marked by the desire to put African merchants at the same level as European firms and private operators, the period under analysis here is characterized by the transfer into African hands of infrastructure and activities that had belonged to Europeans. The *Alhazai* received substantial, formal help from the state, especially after the establishment of the new government following the coup d'état of April 15, 1974.

Trade in Manufactures

The main conduits through which manufactured goods reached the market were the wholesalers, who obtained their supplies from Copro-Niger (for the items over which it held a monopoly), from the European import-export firms, or directly from the world market, assuming import authorizations were available from the government.

Copro-Niger

Between 1962 and 1969 Copro-Niger was in the retail business; in 1969 it was restructured because it had lost so much money through bad management and theft. Retailing was abandoned in favor of wholesaling in an attempt to clean up the organization and prevent future misconduct. The private merchants who had been obtaining goods from Copro-Niger were required to register with the government and to prove Nigerien nationality, although foreigners could obtain special permits to engage in trade within Niger.

These measures considerably limited the number of distributors accredited to deal with the company; other than CFAO and CNF (CNF renamed Niger-Afrique), one Levantine merchant and three Nigeriens received accreditation in 1969. In 1970, three other local entrepreneurs were added to the list, which brought the total to nine.[26] They were selected on the basis of financial qualifications. "We chose the best," a former official of Copro-Niger told me. The selection of *Alhaji* Moussa is an indication of his meaning.[27]

Alhaji Moussa had been a dependent (*bara*) of *Alhaji* Maman dan Dano (mentioned in Chapter 3). For many years, *Alhaji* Moussa sold assorted items, such as perfumes, clothing, and condiments, for his patron at the market or around town. As tradition demands, his patron (*uban-gida*) eventually made him a sizable gift of appreciation, which allowed him to enter business on his own account. *Alhaji* Moussa then linked up with and gained the confidence of the Europeans working in the large trading houses; he bought percales and other fabrics in bulk, often on credit, and resold them at retail.[28]

In 1950 or thereabouts, the Levantine groundnut trader Elias Issa guaranteed a loan for him from CFAO, which enabled him to open his first shop. His business thrived, and in addition to agents who toured the streets of Maradi selling his wares, *Alhaji* Moussa recruited a network of peddlers who bought cloth from him and resold it at tiny hamlets in the bush. Since they bought at a discount and frequently on credit, they became regular clients.

According to records of the revenue service, *Alhaji* Moussa was Maradi's principal African merchant in 1960, one of the few who paid the *patente*. His business continued to grow during the 1960s, when a great deal of money circulated in town. From 1967 on, it achieved unprecedented growth because so many merchants from northern Nigeria turned to Maradi when their regular sources were cut off by the Biafran war.

In 1969 *Alhaji* Moussa was a logical choice to become one of Copro-Niger's distributors. During fiscal year 1970/1971, he bought merchandise worth 27.6 million CFA francs; in 1974/1975 it was 47.7 million, and in 1979/1980, 49.6 million.[29] In order to pay for these purchases, local banks, especially BDRN, loaned him the money, since Copro-Niger did not extend credit.

Alhaji Moussa, as one of nine distributors accredited by Copro-Niger to distribute its imported goods, supplied a great many merchants from his warehouses. By 1970, these nine were handling distribution of all the products over which Copro-Niger held a monopoly, both foodstuffs (salt, sugar, flour, concentrated milk, powdered coffee, tomato paste, tea) and other goods (jute bags, matches, cigarettes, etc.).

He took advantage of his good fortune to diversify into other operations. Still a distributor for the European firms, he began exporting cigarettes and cloth to Nigeria, investing in real estate, dabbling in the trucking business, and so on. In 1970 the import of cigarettes was an exclusive right of Copro-Niger, the senior officials of which were aware that most of the many thousands of cartons were merely in transit through Maradi in the care of agents on their way to Nigeria, where they ended up in the hands of large operators at Kano, Katsina, Gusau, and Daura. The Nigerian government had created a domestic cigarette manufacturing industry and had instituted protective measures, prohibiting the import of British and US cigarettes. However, Nigerian consumers had little appreciation for the local product (*mai zobe*) and preferred to continue buying foreign cigarettes. Nigerian merchants imported them through Maradi in increasing quantities.

The volume of this trade reached such a high level that Copro-Niger decided to become involved in the trade. The accredited distributors placed orders, guaranteed by the banks (BDRN and BIAO), which Copro-Niger forwarded to foreign suppliers. Delivered to Maradi, the cigarettes were stored in duty-free warehouses operated by the customs service of Niger (which levied a transit tax); then they were loaded onto trucks from Nigeria for smuggling across the border.

In 1971 Copro-Niger handled 26,403 cases of Benson and Hedges at 23,000 CFA francs a case, plus 200 cases of Craven A at 21,000 CFA francs, for a total value of more than 601 million CFA francs. These cigarettes, processed through the duty-free warehouses at Maradi, were imported by six *Alhazai* from Maradi and three merchants from Niamey, who paid half of the value in advance and the balance following delivery.[30] This transshipment business became more and more important: as shown in Table 4.5, revenues for Copro-Niger's Maradi branch doubled between 1970 and 1973. Because the transit business was so lucrative, the number of entrepreneurs accredited to Copro-Niger also increased, as shown in Table 4.6.

Table 4.5   Revenues of Copro-Niger's Maradi Branch (in millions of CFA francs)

Year	Amount
1970/71	1,311.0
1971/72	2,016.0
1972/73	2,683.0
1973/74	2,772.0
1974/75	1,068.0
1975/76	1,124.5
1976/77	682.9
1977/78	740.6
1978/79	671.0
1979/80	1,046.7
1980/81	1,123.4
1981/82	1,647.0
1982/83	2,652.0

Source: Copro-Niger

Table 4.6   Number of Distributors Accredited by Copro-Niger's Maradi Branch

Year	Number
1970/71	9
1972/73	22
1974/75	29
1976/77	42
1978/79	51
1980/81	48
1983/84	44

Source: Copro-Niger

Merchants from Niamey and Zinder joined those in Maradi. The revenues realized from cigarette reexports attained considerable levels; for example, during fiscal year 1972/1973, six merchants recorded sales of more than 100 million CFA francs each, and one of the six, from Maradi, exceeded 280 million CFA francs.

Many *Alhazai* took advantage of this new activity to generate profits, which were limited only by their financial means and the contacts they had nurtured among Nigerians. The trucker *Alhaji* Boubakar was one who made money by this means, but the amount was much less significant than that realized by the first *Alhazai* to have been accredited by Copro-Niger.

Nevertheless, because the trade involved smuggling, it was very susceptible to government countermeasures, which account for the numbers in 1974 and 1975 (Table 4.5), when Nigeria took steps to reinforce border controls, disrupting transshipments for many months.[31] In 1975 Copro-Niger abandoned the cigarette transit business permanently, obliging the *Alhazai* to deal directly with foreign suppliers. The merchants reproached Copro-Niger for its lack of vigor and for the high commissions it had been taking on goods in transit. However, when Copro-Niger abandoned the field to private business, exercising its cigarette monopoly only on sales within Niger, that gave the *Alhazai* a free hand to expand their import-export business.

As Table 4.5 shows, the decision caused a sharp drop in the Maradi branch's revenues; thereafter, the branch concentrated on wholesale trade in basic necessities. Here it also ran into trouble, this time caused by illicit imports from Nigeria. In 1978, for example, large amounts of sugar, matches, and concentrated milk were smuggled into Niger and sold at prices well below Copro-Niger's. In addition, the company suffered from repeated, lengthy shortages that inevitably affected revenues.

In 1977 Copro-Niger reentered retail trade, opening shops in many urban centers in order to compete with private retailers and force them to respect the price ceilings the company had been imposing, in theory at least. (The ceilings affected three types of prices: the transfer price to distributors, the discount price, and the retail price.) By so doing, Copro-Niger hoped to diminish the many irregularities occurring in markets around the country.[32]

Today, Copro-Niger's import trade is concentrated in the hands of a small number of wholesalers who are supported by large networks of distributors and retailers. Table 4.7 shows that in 1977/1978, sales to only nine wholesalers produced 65 percent of the Maradi branch's revenues, one of them buying more than 131 million CFA francs' worth of merchandise. The total is close to that of 1980/1981, when fifteen wholesalers produced 63.5 percent of revenues. Copro-Niger thus operated on a basis scarcely different from that established by the European commercial firms: on the input side it monopolized the import of many products, and on the output side it distributed them among a group of wholesalers whose membership was deliberately kept small. This result of Copro-Niger's 1969 reorganization worked to the advantage of the *Alhazai*.

The European Commercial Houses

The restructuring of commercial activities following independence left gaping holes in the ranks of European companies, progressively excluding these firms from the groundnut trade and from their import monopolies over the distribution of manufactured goods.

Dominique Rega suggests that in recent years the companies have abandoned the countryside to concentrate on wholesales in the towns (they no longer sell at retail) and on imports of hardware, European consumer goods,

Table 4.7 Wholesalers Arranged by Annual Revenues (revenues in millions of CFA francs)

Fiscal Year	1977/1978			1980/1981		
Revenue Class	Number of Wholesalers	Revenues by Class	Number of Percentage	Revenues Wholesalers	by Class	Percentage
100 +	1	132.0	18.85	0	169.6	19.60
50–100	2	131.8	18.82	2	380.1	43.90
20–50	6	192.6	27.51	13	226.8	26.00
10–20	8	117.2	16.76	16	89.8	10.50
Under 10	36	126.5	18.06	17		
Total	53	700.1	100.00	48	866.3	100.00

automobiles, trucks, and spare parts rather than exports.[33] At present only two still have branches at Maradi, SCOA having given up. The two are CFAO and Niger-Afrique (formerly CNF), which are supplied from head offices at Niamey that also handle their financial affairs.

The CFAO operates two wholesale/retail outlets, one handling food and drink, fabrics, electrical appliances, and so on, and the other handling hardware and construction materials. The firm obtains some of its inventory from Copro-Niger and the rest using import licenses. It shares with Niger-Afrique an import monopoly on Dutch fabrics (usually colorful cotton prints). Local distributors, who stock up at CFAO for resale at retail, generate most of its revenues.

Niger-Afrique now does wholesale business only, having abandoned retailing. It handles mostly Dutch fabrics, alcoholic beverages, construction materials, and housewares. Two-thirds of its revenues come from fabric sales (see Table 4.9). The fabrics are of exceptional quality, very popular in Niger for making clothing. The *Alhazai* are the branch's main clients for fabrics. They buy at wholesale and resell in their own shops or via intermediaries. (Much of the fabric is reexported to Nigeria.) Like Copro-Niger, the branch does most of its business through a few individuals, ten of whom produced half of its total revenues for fiscal year 1981. In that year also, *Alhaji Moussa* bought 55 million CFA francs' worth of merchandise from the company; this made him one of its biggest customers.

Although the activity of the European firms has diminished in recent years, it would be even less today were they not benefiting from their shared monopoly over the import of Dutch fabrics.

Imports from Nigeria

Eventually, the *Alhazai* obtained authorization to import a certain number of products directly. This licensing system allowed supplemental imports of goods either under state monopoly or simply needed in the economy, including cement, iron, and gasoline.

The method for issuing licenses is worth examining briefly. In theory, they are made available through invitations for bids, followed by contracts between the government and importers. In practice, import licenses are often obtained through political influence; this was true especially during

Table 4.8 Revenues of Niger-Afrique, Maradi Branch (in millions of CFA francs)

Year	Revenues
1979	385
1980	478
1981	650

the administration of President Diori Hamani. Without a doubt, certain *Alhazai* close to the earlier government benefited from political links that favored their commercial enterprises. They obtained authorizations for imports or exports (of livestock and cowpeas) as well as large purchase contracts from the government. For example, *Alhaji* Saley was selected, thanks to support from a high official, to supply millet to the Nigerien army; this produced a substantial income for him over time. *Alhaji* Ali, an active member of the PPN/RDA and a regional official, had use of government facilities by virtue of his political functions and also received orders for providing uniforms; a former tailor, he set up several shops around town to fill the orders.[34]

It appears that those *Alhazai* who were closely allied to the former government experienced some slight decline in their operations after its fall.[35] Others, by contrast, benefited from the new government's measures that favored Nigerien nationals, and from its increasing revenues due to uranium exports. In addition, official trade licenses made smuggling much easier, since a single license might be used fraudulently many times.

Imports from Nigeria consisted of food products, clothing, construction materials, and machinery.

As Table 4.9 shows, food products occupied first place among imports at the end of 1977. It appears they are still the import of choice, given the quantities of rice and sorghum imported in 1981 in order to supply the OPVN. Construction materials (cement, steel reinforcing rods and beams, tiles, etc.) also remain important purchases to meet the needs of the many local builders. The machinery and assorted materials category comprises bicycles, motorbikes, automobiles, special-purpose vehicles, machine tools, and other goods. Nigeria plays an important role in meeting Maradi's needs for these goods as well. As for clothing, in 1977, 91 percent of that category consisted of plastic sandals, which have invaded the local market in recent years to the detriment of traders in traditional leather shoes.

Table 4.9 Imports by Product Category, fourth quarter 1977

Type of Product	Amount (in CFA francs)	Percentage
Food products	34,808,810	48
Clothing	8,069,020	11
Construction materials	18,709,263	26
Machinery and assorted materials	11,096,410	15
Total	72,683,503	100

Source: Maradi Customs Office, cited in Sabo, "Perspectives d'évolution des activités commerciales"

Local importers sometimes specialize in a specific type of product, such as construction materials, fuels, or food products. The state enterprises turn to them to supplement their supplies, providing them special authorizations. In 1972 a single merchant imported wheat flour and sugar worth 25 million CFA francs on behalf of Copro-Niger.

Aside from these official imports, smuggling is important, although usually it involves many trips carrying small quantities. For example, sugar, salt, and tea are often brought in from Nigeria and then sold at prices below those charged at Copro-Niger, which holds import monopolies. Similarly, large quantities of gasoline from Nigeria, where the price is much lower, are smuggled in and sold at prices far below official levels.

The smuggling extends to traditional items. Women bring in large amounts of illicit cola nuts, which are retailed in town. Likewise, the men bring in leaf tobacco, which, like cola nuts, has been a favorite item with traders since the nineteenth century, when it was brought in by mule from the area around Katsina, where it is grown, to Zinder, Agadez, and other towns. The traders also buy various local products, including natron, which they sell as far away as southern Nigeria (Abeakuta, Ibadan, Ilorin). They then return with cola nuts bought at Lagos, thus completing the commercial cycle. These activities are more and more frequently pursued by Nigerien merchants from Maradi, Zinder, and Agadez, who travel to northern Nigerian markets to buy leaf tobacco.[36] They import it into Niger via trails through the bush.

Imports from Nigeria play an important role in Maradi's economy. The proximity of that country and the frequency of communications between Maradi and Kano are among the town's most important assets.

The Growth of Trade with Nigeria

Changes in customs receipts collected at Maradi are an interesting indicator of the growth of commercial exchanges with Nigeria. Figure 4.4 shows one increase beginning in 1967 and ending in 1970; this period corresponds to the Biafran war that cut northern Nigeria's communication links with the sea. When the merchants in Kano and other large northern Nigerian towns found it difficult to obtain imports, they turned to Maradi for agricultural products (cowpeas, meat) and manufactured goods, especially bales of frippery from the United States. At the outset, imports of frippery were monopolized by a single merchant, who also supplied part of northern Nigeria, realizing very high profits in the process. Today he is one of the richest *Alhazai* in Maradi.

The end of the civil war (1970) allowed Nigeria to reestablish normal commercial links, and by 1971 trade with Maradi had fallen to about its prewar level. In 1972 and 1973 customs receipts began to rise again, in part

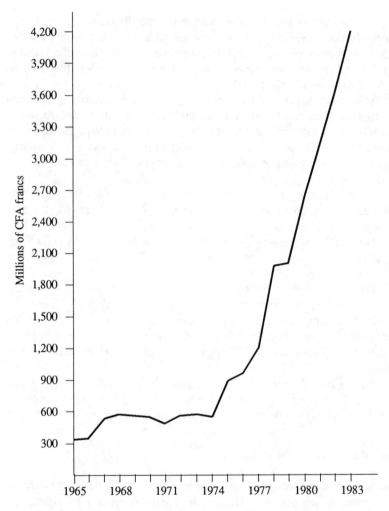

Figure 4.4   Variation in Maradi's Customs Receipts, 1965–1983
Source: Maradi Customs Office

because the drought caused much livestock to be exported and in part because the cigarette trade was getting under way. The latter business grew during 1974 and was joined by increasingly important transit shipments of embroidered fabrics and polyesters. The growth in transit trade was so strong that customs receipts tripled between 1971 and 1977, from 415 million to 1.39 billion CFA francs. By 1977, the total value of goods in transit— consisting primarily of cigarettes and cloth—exceeded 10 billion CFA francs, as shown in Table 4.10.

Table 4.10 Goods in Transit, February–December 1977

Product	Amount (in millions of CFA francs)	Percentage
Cigarettes	4,028.0	40.25
Cloth	5,564.5	55.50
Leaf tobacco	281.0	2.75
Used clothing	132.0	1.50
Dry cell batteries	7.2	—
Total	10,012.7	100.00

Source: Maradi Customs Office, cited in Sabo, "Perspectives d'évolution des activités commerciales"

Although transit trade declined during 1978 and 1979 because of a strengthening of border controls by the Nigerian authorities, it resumed its growth in 1980 and 1981, generating 70 to 80 percent of Maradi's customs receipts.

Transit Trade During the 1970s and 1980s

Since Copro-Niger's retrenchment, transit agents have acted as intermediaries between the importers (the *Alhazai*) and the customs service of Niger. The system works in the following way: the importers, having transmitted an order (for example, for cigarettes or cloth) to their foreign suppliers, turn over to the transit agent responsibility for administrative formalities and commercial transactions. The agents take care of shipping the goods from Cotonou or Lomé and delivering them to customs clearance warehouses at Maradi, where they may not remain more than twenty-one days.[37]

As soon as the customs formalities are finished, the goods are picked up by truckers from Nigeria, who drive them to their destination on the other side of the border, a risky operation because they are violating an official prohibition. In theory, whenever violations are detected, the truck and its cargo are burned. In practice, seizures are rare, since the merchants and Nigerian customs officials negotiate an "arrangement" in advance.

The transit agents, once the operation has been terminated in Niger, report the various transport costs and administrative charges and receive their commissions. There are now three such agencies in Maradi: Nitra, Transcap, and Intertrans. The latter two are distinctly minor players. Nitra is a mixed government–private ownership company created in 1974; it has 100 million CFA francs in equity capital, 65 percent of which is held by Nigerien government entities (Société Nationale des Transports du Niger, or SNTN; Copro-Niger; BDRN; Organisation Commune Bénin-Niger; Nigelec; etc.) and 35 percent by the Société Commerciale des Ports d'Afrique de l'Ouest

(SOCOPAO, a French firm established during the colonial period), which at one time had an agency at Maradi.

Nitra handles virtually every aspect of transit. It takes charge of merchandise at the port or railhead, turns it over to OCDN or to private truckers, clears it through customs, and arranges warehousing and maintenance of the goods. At the government of Niger's insistence, it handles only a very limited class of goods, now moving only cloth imported from the Netherlands, Germany, Japan, and Austria; cigarettes from the United States and Great Britain; leaf tobacco from Malawi and the United States; and frippery from the United States. Table 4.11 indicates the size of its operations.

Nitra acts as agent for the importers in Niger who are the suppliers to Nigeria's largest merchants. It is impossible to do a specific, detailed study of the links between the merchants of Maradi and those of Nigeria.[38] However, it appears that the *Alhazai* take part in networks centered in Nigeria. The very wealthy entrepreneurs of Kano once supplied capital to their representatives in Niger (and still do, according to one informant); at the beginning of the transit business, the participants on the Niger side lacked the funds to place really large orders abroad, even when they were able to obtain some financing from local banks. It is therefore probable that the *Alhazai* had—and some of them still have—patrons in Nigeria. It also appears that one of the principal importers in Maradi acts partly in his own name and partly as a front for merchants in Nigeria. The Nigerians order merchandise in Europe, the United States, and Asia using the name of this *Alhaji*, who assumes administrative responsibility for the operation. They supply all the money and pay him a commission. The profit margins of the importers in Niger are set in negotiations with the Nigerians. Given the secrecy of these transactions, they are hard to evaluate precisely, but the margins are probably in the range of 4 to 6 percent (more in exceptional cases); these rates mean substantial total

Table 4.11 Annual Tonnages Billed by Nitra

Fiscal Year	Tonnages Billed
1974/75	5,330
1975/76	14,600
1976/77	11,590
1977/78	21,103
1978/79	24,300
1979/80	18,020
1980/81	18,600

Source: Nitra Agency, Maradi

earnings for the *Alhazai* by virtue of the revenues involved, the more so given that the business requires neither investment in infrastructure nor personnel.

As Table 4.12 reveals, importers' combined revenues represent a very important sum, more than 19 billion CFA francs in a single year. At Maradi, there are at most a dozen such importers; other than the *Alhazai* there are two Levantine merchants whose role is far from negligible. All these importers are in fact distributors for major international cigarette manufacturers, who deal regularly with them and have representatives based in the large ports (Cotonou, Lomé).

In Niger these traders benefit from special authorizations to engage in transit trade.[39] They are supported by the banks, which lend them up to 50 percent of the value of their orders.[40] They deal either directly with their Nigerian clients or through subcontracting with other local merchants, whose means are limited, even though they, too, have links to Nigeria.

Transit trade is clearly the basis for the wealth of leading *Alhazai*, who, in contrast to their neighbors in Zinder, have demonstrated a remarkable dynamism in establishing close lines of communication with the Hausa merchants of Kano, Katsina, Gusau, and Kaduna. However, this wealth rests upon fragile foundations, since transit trade is, in essence, smuggling, which succeeds only because the Nigerian authorities tolerate it. Thus, "it could all collapse from one day to the next," according to an informant, particularly if the federal government were to yield to pressures from Nigerian merchants, who want import licenses, access to hard currency, and abolition of protectionist measures intended to bolster Nigerian industries. The route through Niger would become useless, causing severe repercussions for

Table 4.12 Revenues of Several Importers at Maradi, fiscal year 1979/80 (in millions of CFA francs)

Importer	Revenues
1	2,352.26
2	6,278.85
3	316.76
4	4,643.68
5	722.76
6	2,145.84
7	237.14
8	2,363.23
9	230.80
Total	19,291.32

Maradi's economy. Although such measures have not been adopted, Nigeria's recent closing of the borders to overland traffic (May 1984) appears to have diminished transit shipments without completely stopping them. It is too early to estimate what effects the closing will have if it is prolonged, but since 1975, the transit business has provided the *Alhazai* important profits, and the measures taken by Nigeria so far do not appear to have put an end to them because the frontier, even though officially closed, is quite permeable.[41]

The Movement of Imports and Exports

In addition to transit, other trade with Nigeria involves high volumes and a great variety of products. Niger's imports consist mainly of food products (tomato paste, cornmeal, crackers, rice, millet, sorghum), cloth and clothing, construction materials, machinery, and petroleum products. Exports include agricultural products (cowpeas, onions) and livestock.

Studies of road traffic conducted in 1976–1977 show that the Maradi region has a trade deficit: it brings in more than it ships out.[42]

The figures in Table 4.13 reflect only part of the merchandise trade between the two countries, since smuggling is rampant. There are countless trails in the bush, far from the main roads, that carry truck traffic intent on avoiding the customs checkpoints.

Export smuggling involves very high tonnages of cowpeas, as well as livestock walked across the border on the hoof. Import smuggling includes Nigerian industrial products of all kinds, food products over which Copro-Niger holds an import monopoly (such as sugar, salt, or tea), and even cigarettes: some of the British and US cigarettes exported to Nigeria in the transit trade are smuggled back into Niger, where, because the smugglers have not paid any taxes, they are sold more cheaply than the same brands carrying the official stamp, "For sale in Niger."

Whether via the official or the parallel market, the Maradi region is a net exporter of agricultural products, playing a significant role in supplying Nigeria. In return, the region is a major importer of manufactured goods.

Table 4.13 Merchandise Traffic at the Dan Issa Border Post, 1977 (in metric tons)

Direction	Quantity
Imports	28,000
Exports	21,500
Total	49,500

Foreign Exchange Speculations

Ever since the beginning of colonization, when the Europeans introduced their currency to replace the cowrie shell used locally, there has been cross-border traffic based on differences in prices for merchandise. For example, at one time groundnuts fetched higher prices in Nigeria, and part of the crop harvested on the Nigerien side of the border was marketed there. After 1953, the flow reversed because France set groundnut prices for Niger that were above world market levels; great quantities of northern Nigerian groundnuts were smuggled into Niger. Today, prices are higher in Nigeria once again, so part of the Nigerien harvest ends up in Nigeria.[43]

Speculation based upon price differentials continues today, usually by merchant specialists (in cowpeas, for example) who are difficult to arrest even though the customs officers know who they are. Beyond question, their traffic is as important as regular legal trade; it ranges from exports of agricultural products, whose prices are lower in Niger, to imports of manufactured goods, which are cheaper in Nigeria.

The price differentials between the two countries for similar merchandise depend in large measure upon the rate of exchange between the Nigerian naira and the CFA franc. The nonconvertibility of the naira on world financial markets makes it difficult for Nigerian entrepreneurs to buy hard currencies; this has given birth to a parallel market in which the Nigerian currency is discounted from its official value. In 1981, 1 naira was worth 423 CFA francs at the bank, whereas it was worth only 318 CFA francs at the parallel market rate.

This game involving two naira exchange rates, official and unofficial, creates fruitful opportunities for speculation, and a great many people play it to one degree or another.[44] Today this extremely lucrative game appears to be dominated by a single *Alhaji,* who extends credit to his many intermediaries around town and at the market. It is also played in Nigeria, where merchants can buy from speculators the CFA francs they otherwise would have to obtain (at high rates) from the banks.

In 1970 exchange rate manipulations allowed a handful of operators to realize extraordinary gains. At the time, the civil war in Nigeria had just ended, and the country was importing enormous quantities of meat and cowpeas. As Guy Nicolas observed,

> The governments of Niger and Nigeria concluded an accord to promote exports from the former country to the latter. At that point, the Nigerian pound had just undergone a steep devaluation. Under the accord's terms, the government of Niger agreed to purchase Nigerian currency at the old exchange rate (i.e., 35 CFA francs per shilling instead of 25, or 700 CFA francs per pound instead of 500). Moreover, the actual transactions were inflated by fictitious exports: the rich merchants at Kano provided their Nigerien accomplices large amounts of money ostensibly to pay for purchase of goods, and the customs tariffs were paid and documented. This scam generated a profit of 10

CFA francs per shilling, 200 per pound, or 400,000 per million CFA francs officially exchanged. The revenue was divided among the partners. Certain merchants at Maradi acquired tens of millions of CFA francs in this way over a period of weeks. Thanks to this operation, one man was able to repay a debt of 1.2 million CFA francs to a state-owned credit institution.[45]

The "pea scandal," as it was known around Maradi, enriched several *Alhazai*, who today are among the wealthiest people in town.

Aside from such speculations, black market variations in the naira–CFA franc exchange rate produce other important economic effects upon Maradi and the surrounding countryside.[46] In 1978, 1 naira was worth about 200 CFA francs; by 1982 it had reached 318 CFA francs. Thus, products imported from Nigeria cost more. This squeezed profit margins for the traders, who were unable to recoup all of the price increase by passing it along to consumers, whose purchasing power had not increased commensurately. According to several local officials, there was a slowdown in the economy at the time, and since Nigeria could not supply all the Maradi region's needs, Niamey intervened in a substantial way.[47]

The impressive gains realized on the one hand thanks to the volume of trade with Nigeria and on the other thanks to local sales (manufactured goods, grains, etc.) were often reinvested in real estate or the transport business, which were also very lucrative activities.

Real Estate Markets

As noted earlier, the revenue service tripled the amount of taxes it collected on improved real property between 1960 and 1970 (Table 3.6). This growth in real estate tax receipts is explained not merely by improvements in tax collection (better records of building construction) but also in large part by the expansion of the groundnut trade and by the way the town responded to its demographic growth.

At that time new construction (warehouses, office buildings, etc.) appears to have been more the work of Nigerien state institutions (in firms such as Sonara, Copro-Niger, and BDRN) or foreign investors (such as Sonitan and Siconiger) than of *Alhazai*, who were making only minor investments by building market stalls.

Beginning in 1971, real estate activity expanded rapidly (Table 3.6), this time under the influence of *Alhazai* who were accumulating large sums from wholesale business with Copro-Niger and from the transit trade. They built many villas, not only at Maradi but also at Niamey and Zinder; some of them owned more than ten. The villas were rented to the government as housing for officials (Nigeriens or expatriates) or to various companies and international organizations, especially at Niamey, where rents were very high.

In addition to building villas, as of 1974 they were buying business assets, including buildings, from European and other firms long established at Maradi.[48] As a result, they acquired the property of SCOA, Niger-Afrique, Ruetsch, and Dumoulin, which had been the symbols of the colonial trade economy. One *Alhaji* bought from a European an entire block of buildings at the center of town, including a cinema, a hotel/bar/restaurant, shops, and dwellings, while another built a second cinema and a modern hotel.

The shift of investment into real property (Table 3.6) continues today with the construction of many villas in the residential neighborhoods.[49] Such investments constitute one of the principal methods for building capital as well as a source of regular income. (Villas were renting for more than 100,000 CFA francs per month in 1983.) As one European, a longtime resident of Maradi, says, "If groundnuts built the town, commerce with Copro-Niger and the transit trade have allowed not only its continuing development but also a gradual transfer of control over the local economy from Europeans and import-export houses to the *Alhazai*, with encouragement from the government of Niger—certainly since the coup d'état in 1974."

In any case, the *Alhazai* have invested a large share of their capital in real estate. That it is safe and feasible helps explain this choice, but above all they want real estate ownership because the ability to obtain bank loans depends upon having land titles to offer as collateral. The two local banks strongly supported the *Alhazai's* activities by giving them numerous credit facilities, which were extended easily and cheaply early on, and later more stringently because of substantial arrears by some of the merchants. Since then the banks have demanded collateral (real estate titles or other assets) before making loans; this has led the merchants to invest in real property. Land titles are prerequisite for borrowing money, making them indispensable for those *Alhazai* who wish to pursue activities that require bank credit— namely, the transit trade.

According to information provided by one of the banks, they are unable to resell any villas seized through foreclosure; since there is a certain solidarity among the *Alhazai*, no one will buy such properties.

Transportation

In addition to real property, the *Alhazai* have made many investments in the transport business. They consider such activities even more attractive for investment purposes than real estate. Ever since the 1950s, whenever one of them has been able to accumulate a bit of money from groundnut marketing or selling manufactured goods, he has bought (usually on credit) a truck with which to do business in different parts of the region, even in the most remote towns, such as Madaoua and Tahoua.

Merchandise Transport

The groundnut trade, Opération Hirondelle in particular, led to the development of the trucking industry, which was monopolized for a long time by a few European individual operators (such as Vignat and Garcia, A. Paul, F. Balay, P. Goussanou, and S. Bourgy) or big firms (Compagnie Transafricaine, Compagnie Transsaharienne). In 1960 there were few African truckers because only those with very good connections to the commercial houses could afford to buy a truck.

After independence, the government of Niger encouraged nationals to go into transport (offering bank credit facilities and contracts with state companies) and allowed them to build up their truck fleets in order to participate in groundnut hauling, as described in the biographical sketch of *Alhaji* Boubakar in Chapter 3. Beginning in 1970, truckers in Maradi began to get sizable subcontracts from SNTN to take part in building the mining facilities in the Aïr region. Traffic between Parakou and Arlit was heavy and profitable. It continues today, although SNTN has built up its fleet and rarely subcontracts work any more.

The drought of 1974 helped the truckers as well.[50] As soon as it seized power in April of that year, the military government organized a campaign for a "return to the home village" in order to send back to the bush the many people who had taken refuge in the towns. For this purpose the government rented trucks from the private truckers, each load of refugees being accompanied by a truckload of food.[51] The twenty-one food distribution centers, spread over the entire *département*, were also supplied regularly from Maradi. The growth of trade with Nigeria also favored the truckers, filling the roads between Parakou and Maradi. Some truckers work closely with the Organisation Commune Bénin-Niger (OCBN), which is responsible for moving the merchandise.

Finally, some individuals have invested heavily in specialized equipment (construction machinery, dump trucks, etc.) that is leased to construction firms or organizations such as the Projet de Développement Rural de Maradi. Since it came into being in 1976, the latter entity has used equipment to build irrigation canals in the Maradi River valley near Maradi and for various other infrastructural projects.[52]

In 1980 the records of the revenue service listed fifty-four truckers, of whom eight accounted for 46 percent of the local fleet. Thus, the activity was concentrated in the hands of a few individuals, one of whom had skillfully built up his business to the point where he had several locations, not only in Maradi and Niamey but also in Nigeria.

Passenger Transportation

Maradi is a crossroads: the transport terminal, where bush taxis come and go constantly, is one of the liveliest places in town. A study done in 1976–1977 shows that the most-frequented route is the one linking Maradi with

Nigeria.[53] In second place is traffic on the road to Guidan-Roumji, that is, in the direction of Niamey.

Transport of passengers, which is less lucrative than transport of merchandise, is divided among a multitude of individuals because it requires a smaller capital investment. It increased substantially with the modernization of Niger's road network, which has improved steadily thanks to the revenues that the state has received from exploitation of the uranium deposits. Maradi is now linked by paved roads to Niamey, Zinder, and Nigeria and by unpaved laterite tracks to each of the administrative subcenters of the region.

The weakness of public transportation, which serves only the main routes, has given rise to many small carriers who provide regular service between Maradi and other towns. The number of taxis increased rapidly, from fewer than ten in 1978 to ninety-four in 1980. A very profitable activity, the taxi business has attracted both merchants and civil servants as investors: they rent vehicles to the drivers, who pay a fixed amount per day.

Conclusion

The 1960s saw a sharp change in the development of Maradi, a change brought on by its involvement in the world economy: its activity shifted from the regional or national to the international scale. The town now plays an important economic role in Niger, acting as a counterweight to the preponderance of Niamey; it has also overtaken its rival, Zinder. Maradi is a young city, dynamic but also a bit fragile in its prosperity, as no one knows what will happen if Nigeria modifies its legislation and gives its businesses free access to foreign currencies and world markets.

Maradi's lively economy is popularly identified with the *Alhazai*. They constitute a privileged social class whose economic power is well established. The wealthy merchants took advantage of favorable circumstances: the war in Biafra, then the coming to power in 1974 of a new government determined to stimulate the national economy, and, finally, rapidly growing state revenues from uranium exports. They were able to exploit these events because of support from the banks, which at first lent very generously, although later more prudently.[54] Without the banks, their accumulation of wealth would not have been so rapid.

Figure 4.5 illustrates the diversification achieved by two particularly successful *Alhazai*: commerce in manufactured goods, transit trade, speculation in foreign exchange, transportation, real estate, production and marketing of farm and livestock products, lending at interest, and investment in company shares.

In addition to the nobility, the *Alhazai* today include the following names: *Alhaji* Maman Djitao, *Alhaji* Gonda Garki, *Alhaji* Balla dan Sani, *Alhaji* Issuhou Guizo, *Alhaji* Mani Gourgou, *Alhaji* Balla Kalto, *Alhaji* Andoumé, *Alhaji* Zinguilé, and *Alhaji* Yahaya Ardé. These merchants have

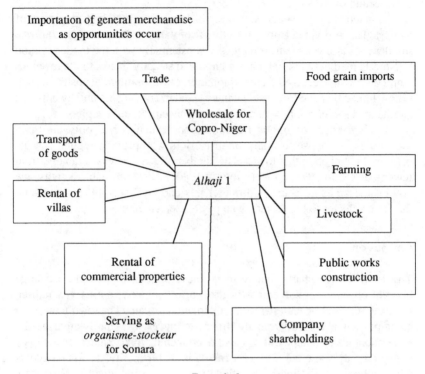

Example 1

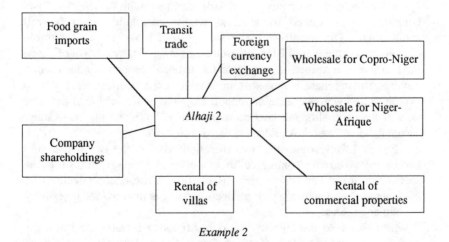

Example 2

Figure 4.5   Business Diversification by Two Major *Alhazai*

made their fortunes recently, supplanting the *Alhazai* who obtained their wealth from the groundnut trade. Few of the men just named were involved in the groundnut business; instead, during the colonial period and afterwards they took part to one degree or another in the distribution of manufactured goods. This reinforces the hypothesis that the latter was more profitable than the trade in groundnuts.[55]

As the typology of merchants in Chapter 5 shows, there are few grand successes, the majority of merchants being involved in modest, not to say mediocre, operations. Maradi, however, the city of *Alhazai*, is measured by the success of the richest among them.

OTHER URBAN ECONOMIC ACTIVITIES

Over the course of a decade, Maradi became a birthplace for industries, although they were not strong enough to occupy the central position long held by commercial activity. Industry emerged alongside the commercial sector during the 1970s. The purpose of the first industries, introduced by the French during the colonial period, was to process agropastoral products (groundnuts, cotton, skins) for export. The expansion of industry after 1974 is explainable in large measure by the intervention of the Nigerien state, whose resources were considerably augmented by exploitation of the uranium deposits in the Aïr Mountains.[56] The production facilities put in place during 1970–1971 were intended to reduce Niger's imports and make the country less dependent on foreign sources. Besides the state, companies with mixed state-private ownership played an important role in creating new enterprises. Many private investors, notably the *Alhazai*, took part in the formation of new firms.

Aside from the growth of an industrial sector, the process of urbanization was accompanied by the appearance of many small activities that, in the cities of the Third World, constitute what economists call the "informal" sector. It comprises a great variety of occupations, such as traditional crafts, small processing industries, and microcommerce. Its principal characteristics vary from one African city to another, but its economic role is important for several reasons:

- It provides most of the employment in the urban setting, which means that unemployment need not rise as fast as the population increases caused by rural migration and demographic growth. It offers an alternative to employment in the modern sector, such as industry or government.
- Its production and circulation of goods represents increased financial and material activity since it meets some of the population's economic needs.

- It forms a transitional bridge between the rural sector, from which most of the workers come, and the capitalist sector; that is, it transforms and adapts laborers so that they become employable by the capitalists. This phenomenon is encountered in all the big cities.

The Emergence of an Industrial Sector

The industrial and informal sectors have developed parallel to the commercial sector. There are four categories of industrial enterprise in Maradi: processing of agropastoral products, extractive processing, manufacturing, and construction and public works. Table 4.14 provides basic data on the industrial firms.

Processors of Agropastoral Products

There are four enterprises in this group: the vegetable oil mill belonging to Siconiger, the cotton gin operated by CFDT, Sonitan's tannery, and the fruit processor, Conco-Niger.

Siconiger. Because its history is outlined in Chapter 3, it suffices to add that the 1971–1972 farm season marked the apogee of its activity, followed by a steady decline paralleling that of groundnut production. For example, in 1980–1981 the company was in operation for only about two weeks, during which it processed 1,500 metric tons of groundnuts despite having a capacity of 45,000 metric tons.

In order to avoid closing the oil mill entirely, which would cost its personnel their jobs, Siconiger obtained a license to import refined soybean oil. By mixing four parts of soybean oil to one part of groundnut oil,

Table 4.14 Industrial Firms in Maradi

Firm	Year Created	Capital[a]	Employees (1983)	Revenues[a] (1983)	Payroll[a] (1983)
Siconiger	1942	400.00	85	2,144.00	55.65
Sonitan	1970	52.20	92	695.00	67.00
Sonibri	1977	90.10	100[b]	161.00	50.40
Fabmétal	1974	50.00	37	164.00	23.90
Unimo	1976	10.00	31	186.48	18.18
Sonifac	1977	100.00	108[c]	216.00	69.00
Séfamag	1975	1.12	13[b]	34.20	11.40[b]
Conco-Niger	1979	n/a	13[b]	11.30	4.96[b]
Braniger	1981	1,916.00	88	1,475.00	42.76

Notes: [a]Millions of CFA francs   [b]As of 1980   [c]As of 1981

Siconiger was able to sell about 3,150 metric tons of oil in 1981. This solution, however, did not resolve the company's problems, which included loss of technicians due to lack of raw materials and inability to meet the needs of the Nigerien market, which now imports vegetable oil.

The Compagnie Française du Développement des Textiles. The CFDT cotton gin, built in 1956, saw intense activity during the 1960s, but after the drought, cotton planting was neglected in favor of more profitable grain production. Purchases of cotton at the gin in Maradi, which reached 1,800 metric tons in 1969–1970, fell to less than 200 metric tons in 1978–1979. This reduction in activity led to the closing of the gin in 1980, although its infrastructure remains in place.

The Société Nigérienne de Tannerie. Sonitan was created in 1970, with a capital of 52.2 million CFA francs, a majority of it of foreign origin. Its purpose is production of raw, semifinished, and finished skins. The raw material is the Maradi russet goat (known abroad as the Sokoto goat), whose skin makes a leather of very high quality.

At one time, these skins were the object of intense trade between this part of Niger and Nigeria. As a result of the urging and advice of a veterinarian assigned at Maradi in the early 1950s, the governor of Niger closed the border with Nigeria to trade in hides and skins and persuaded the commercial houses to become involved in this activity (building slaughterhouses, drying sheds, etc.). The CNF, which had close ties with the British firm Unilever, one of the major leather-processing firms, was among the first to invest.

Siconiger also decided to become involved, using its network of groundnut collectors. The success of this step led to the founding of the Union Commerciale du Niger, a company created uniquely to collect and export hides and skins. The UCN operated from 1957 until 1970, when it was voluntarily dissolved because its shareholders wanted to participate in Sonitan.

The new firm grew very rapidly at first, especially in 1972–1973, when a great many animals died from the drought. Sonitan collected skins for its own account until the creation, in 1972, of the Société Nigérienne des Cuirs et des Peaux (SNCP), which now has a trade monopoly permitting it to supply Sonitan and Sotapo, a similar firm located at Zinder.

Capacity of the tannery at Maradi is 850,000 skins a year. In 1983 its production was 833,000 skins, exported mostly to France and Italy, although part of the output is now used in Niger itself. Sonitan has one of the best performance records of any local firm: a profit of 17 million CFA francs before taxes in 1983.

Conco-Niger. This small enterprise makes jams, fruit juices, and syrups. Started in 1979 through the initiative of an individual supported financially by the Sudan Interior Mission (the US Protestant group), it has thirteen employees. It regularly buys fruit from farmers in the Maradi River valley near Maradi and sells its output (20,000 jars of jam in 1980) in the urban centers. Financial problems closed the factory in 1983, and no solution to them has been found thus far.

These four enterprises are very dependent upon agropastoral production; any disaster that affects the sector inevitably strikes them, too. The cases of Siconiger and CFDT are illustrations.

Extractive Industries

There is only one extractive operation in Maradi: the Société Nigérienne de Briquetterie (Sonibri), created in 1976 with an initial capital of 300 million CFA francs, of which the majority was provided by BDRN, and the rest by local *Alhazai*. The company has a factory at Djirataoua, about 10 kilometers south of Maradi. It extracts clay from a quarry and produces bricks for construction and decoration. Its modern German equipment has a capacity of 4 million bricks a year. The enterprise encountered financial difficulties in 1979 and 1980; its recovery program failed, and it closed its doors in 1983, although the infrastructure remains in place.

Processing Industries

There are five processing plants: two for construction metalwork (Séfamag and Fabmétal), one that makes foam mattresses (Unimo), one that manufactures textiles (Sonifac), and one that produces beer and soft drinks (Braniger).

Séfamag. A small firm that manufactures ox-drawn carts and similar equipment for farmers who use draft animals, Séfamag was started in 1975 with very little capital (1.2 million CFA francs) by Nigerien workers trained at the Protestant mission. Its production equipment is inadequate and its personnel very few: eleven persons in 1981. That year it achieved 42.8 million CFA francs in revenues. At 960 carts in 1981, production was far below capacity (5,000 carts) because of inability to build up sufficient inventories of raw materials. This, in turn, was caused by a lack of working capital, a common problem of small producing enterprises.

This particular firm should be modernized and provided greater resources, inasmuch as demand for farm equipment is certain to increase in coming years. Séfamag would also do better to devote itself to private clients and to stop working almost exclusively for the government's Union Nigérienne de Crédit et de Coopération.

As in the case of Conco-Niger, the Sudan Interior Mission played a decisive role in the creation of Séfamag. With an approach that combines liberalism (encouraging the emergence of small entrepreneurs) and charity (training workers and providing them jobs), this mission encourages private initiative. It also provides capital, which is otherwise all too often missing at the local level. Despite this, both enterprises have encountered financial difficulties because they operate according to Western organizational precepts that have not been adapted to a developing country such as Niger.

Fabmétal. Created in 1974, this firm had an initial capital of 50 million CFA francs held entirely by Nigeriens of Levantine origin, who had got their start in the groundnut trade. It manufactures metal products such as beds, tables, chairs, armoires, and office furniture. Its materials—tubes, sheet metal, hardware—are imported from Nigeria, Belgium, Great Britain, and Japan. Although Fabmétal enjoyed good beginnings, its situation has steadily deteriorated because there now exist a multiplicity of small artisanal workshops, many of whose personnel trained at Fabmétal. Competition from these shops, where output is of inferior quality but is sold at much lower prices, has robbed Fabmétal of its initial market (metal beds) and forced it to diversify in order to survive.[57] From 14,000 beds in 1977, production fell to 4,000 by 1981. Several projects are under study (production of copper for bed frames, bedsprings, etc.) to rejuvenate this firm, whose personnel has diminished by half since 1977 (thirty-seven persons in 1983).

Unimo. The same shareholders who created Fabmétal created Unimo in 1976, subscribing initial capital of 6 million CFA francs. It produces foam mattresses using imported raw materials, thus complementing Fabmétal's activities. The company has a monopoly position in Niger, and its commercial network permits it to serve Niger's various urban centers, particularly the Niamey market. For some time, however, it has been hampered by mattress smuggling from Nigeria and by merchants who buy unfinished mattress foam and cover it with cheaper fabric, selling the result at a price lower than that offered for Unimo's finished products.

At the beginning, Unimo obtained its financial support from Fabmétal, which was in sound condition. In 1982 the situation was reversed: Unimo helped Fabmétal survive a crisis. In recent months Unimo has suffered because of massive smuggling from Nigeria, and its managers are very worried about the future.

The Société Nigérienne de Fabrication de Couvertures. Sonifac was started in 1976; its capital of 100 million CFA francs was held by the government of Niger, two mixed-ownership firms (BDRN and Copro-Niger), and several *Alhazai.* Its purpose was to make blankets out of textile-industry waste products; these were obtained from Nitex, in Niamey, and from abroad (Benin, Côte d'Ivoire, France, and Italy). Its modern equipment gave it a capacity of 350,000 blankets per year.

The firm has been in trouble since its inception because the protective measures taken in its behalf by Copro-Niger (which stopped importing competing products) failed to produce the expected effects. In addition, local wholesalers, including some of Sonifac's shareholders, are not interested in marketing its output. As a result, considerable unsold inventories accumulated. The situation improved in 1981, when the old models were taken off the market and new ones substituted. Soon thereafter, however, quality fell again and the factory was forced to close. A restructuring of the company with additional investment from outside financial participants will be needed before it can reopen; in 1980 it employed 100 people and produced only 57,000 blankets.

Braniger. Maradi's newest enterprise (1981), Braniger was originally intended for Zinder, but that town's water supply problems caused the plant to be built at Maradi. Using imported raw materials, it makes carbonated soft drinks and beer for the regional market consisting of the *départements* of Tahoua, Maradi, Agadez, Zinder, and Diffa. It has an investment capital of 2 billion CFA francs; production capacity is 30,000 hectoliters of soft drinks and 50,000 hectoliters of beer annually, plus 6 metric tons of ice per day. When it opened in 1981 it had seventy employees.

Construction and public works

Long ago the Europeans founded numerous construction firms (Dumoulin, Gautry, Lingois, Georget, Gran, etc.) that divided the construction market among them. Except for Lingois, they all ceased their activities and were replaced by Nigerien firms usually headed by someone trained at one of the French predecessor firms. The example of *Alhaji* Seydou is typical.[58]

Alhaji Seydou was brought to Maradi from the Mayahi area shortly after his birth. At about age fifteen, he became an apprentice mason with a European businessman, Dumoulin. As his qualifications increased (he became a journeyman and then a master mason), he changed jobs repeatedly to take advantage of opportunities. After about fifteen years, he began working informally on his own in 1968, picking up jobs from merchants and government workers. In 1976 he decided to start a regular business. He explains his decision thus: "As an ordinary laborer, I had a lot of problems, because the customers would argue about the price and they paid poorly, sometimes not at all. With my own company, I set my price and the client either agrees or he doesn't. In addition, I can bid on state contracts, so now I'm getting jobs from the government."

Once *Alhaji* Seydou established his firm, government contracting led to his construction of sewers for the town of Maradi, which was a sizable piece of business. Since 1980, however, he has been in financial difficulties, Niger having seen its resources shrink so much that many projects have been frozen. Also, he tried to diversify geographically: he obtained contracts to build dispensaries in the bush, and he tried to set up an office in Tahoua. Despite his best efforts, the recession has hurt him, and he has had to lay off personnel.

The principal Nigerien construction firms today are Sonimap (created in

1974 with a capital of 8 million CFA francs), Lawally Yahaya, the Bagna Mali company, and Soniba (founded in 1977 with a capital of 1 million CFA francs). Competition among them is intense. Each firm tries to cut its costs in order to gain market share, especially with the government. At times a firm will find itself unable to carry out a contract alone and will subcontract a part of it to its competitors or to a jobber.[59] In general, no African construction firm has the equipment or skills available to the state or to European firms operating in Africa (Satom, Dragages, etc.) As a result, African firms fail to get important projects.

Since 1980, the construction market has softened because the state, the principal purchaser, has seen its mining revenues diminish.[60] Therefore, the Maradi firms have tried to get contracts in other urban centers, notably at Tahoua, which has just decided to build a sanitation system and which has few local firms.

As for road construction, the market is dominated by foreign firms and one Nigerien company, Wazir.

Prospects for Industry at Maradi

The description just given shows that after a takeoff period (1974–1977), the town's industry has experienced a series of reverses that led to plant closures (CFDT, Sonibri, Sonifac, and Conco-Niger). These failures are attributable to management errors, sometimes dating back to market analyses in the feasibility study stage (in the case of Sonifac). The fragility of organizations modeled on Western firms contrasts with the robust vigor of the *Alhazai*, who operate in close harmony with local economic and social structures.

Nevertheless, a resurgence in the industrial sector may yet manifest itself thanks to Braniger and, more recently, the Société Nigérienne de Production des Allumettes (Sonipal), a match factory. Future development will depend upon projects now under study, which include factories for making electric batteries, bottled gas, bicycles, and motorbikes; canning tomato concentrate; and shaping aluminum.

Experience shows that the industrialization of a town such as Maradi and a country such as Niger encounters many obstacles, among which are the following:

- Market size is inadequate, as Niger has a small population (less than 6 million) with little purchasing power.
- The cost of inputs, including electricity and fuel, is so high that investors, especially foreigners, are not interested.
- Competition from neighbors, Nigeria in particular, is severe. Nigeria began its industrialization some years ago and is able to produce at costs much lower than those in Niger.
- Transporting exports to foreign markets is expensive. Niger remains an enclave country despite improvements to its road network; transport

to ocean ports such as Cotonou and Lomé is expensive enough to make export of some products to Europe prohibitive.
* Existing social legislation appears to be too strict and too advanced for the country's current level of development. Without a doubt it deters creation of new enterprises, inasmuch as potential investors hesitate out of fear of government interference.

These points do not favor a true industrialization of Niger, whose urban centers in all probability can accommodate only small producers. Still, in that context Maradi has, after Niamey, the best advantages, including the following assets:

* Attractive setting, with substantial unused land resources;
* Good communications, including connections with Niamey, Zinder, and towns in Nigeria;
* Geographic location, making transport costs low because of closeness to other major urban centers;
* Abundant labor reserves because of its well-populated rural areas;
* An attractive market;
* Existing industry and infrastructure, including energy, that can act as magnets for new productive facilities.

Given certain initiatives plus support from potential investors, industrialization may have a future in Maradi. The government of Niger has an essential role to play at two levels: by intervening directly in the creation of enterprises and by enacting legislative measures encouraging private investment (by revising Article 6 of Law 74-19, the investment code, so as to favor small and medium-sized domestic enterprises). Given the right policy and legal situation, there are two categories of potential private investors, Levantines and Nigeriens.

The former got started in the groundnut trade and served Sonara as *organismes-stockeurs*. Since the drought, they have refocused their operations toward investing in industry. For example, the Assad family founded Fabmétal and Unimo. Other families helped start Société Nigérienne du Gypse et de la Cire (Sonigec), which produces gypsum and wax, and Sonipal; both firms have now ceased operating, the first because of economic conditions and the second, ironically, because of a fire.

Levantine entrepreneurs take a strong interest in small industry; they also have capital to invest on both sides of the border. It must be emphasized that their economic role is not inconsiderable (especially in transit trade) and, unlike the Europeans, they are still strongly entrenched at Maradi because they are better integrated into the local milieu, most of them holding Nigerien nationality.

The second group, in particular the *Alhazai*, specialize principally in commercial activities, sources of high and quick profits. For the moment, they are taking only the most timid steps toward investment in industry. These take the form either of a capital investment to help set up a new enterprise (the case with Sonibri, Sonifac, and, more recently, Sonipal) or purchase of shares in an existing company; four *Alhazai* who had long been associated with Siconiger became shareholders in 1984. Perhaps the more distant future will see a class of industrial entrepreneurs such as exists in Europe.[61]

Foreign investors are also permitted to participate in the creation of enterprises; however, their involvement is likely to be limited, given Niger's handicaps.

Under the circumstances, it appears that the role of the Nigerien government is essential to the industrialization of Maradi. With respect to employment, in 1983 the industrial sector (excluding construction and public works) employed fewer than 500 persons, a tiny percentage of the active urban population.[62] This points up a contradiction: industrial firms are often capital intensive and use few workers, whereas low labor costs suggest they should be using less capital and more people. This situation is not limited to Maradi, but is found in other Third World cities: the industrial sector creates few jobs and does little to absorb the urban unemployed, a role that appears to have devolved upon small urban organizations in what is generally described as the "unstructured" or "informal" sector.

The Development of an Informal Sector

Among the few characteristics shared by all microeconomic activities at Maradi are their occasional nature and intermittent revenues. Otherwise the microeconomy is extremely varied in its organization and its products, which Philippe Hugon has assigned to three broad categories:[63]

Services involve exchanges of cash for immediate labor, which can be rendered to persons (personal services) or to objects (material services). Among the former are occupations such as barbers and hairdressers, shoe-shiners, healers, and prostitutes; among the latter, repairmen for all kinds of goods—shoes, clocks and watches, radios, motorbikes, and so on.

Small manufacturing involves the transformation of raw materials into finished products through manual labor using tools (and sometimes using machinery); this can mean reprocessing of used tires and utensils, for example, or making new things such as metal window frames, tailored clothing, pottery, shoes, and woven fabrics.

Microcommerce and transport of merchandise see to the marketing of the products just mentioned. Microretailers include country peddlers, door-to-door peddlers, "table vendors," and shop clerks. [Table vendors sell a great variety of small items (candy, cigarettes, wristwatches, soap, perfume, matches, sunglasses, flashlights, audio cassettes, dry-cell batteries) from small wooden tables that can be carried easily from one street corner to another; they occupy the bottom rung of the urban commercial ladder—Translator.] Transporters include water bearers, barrow pushers, and taxi drivers.

Diversification of Occupations

As the city has grown, occupations have multiplied. Long ago, the occupations making up the traditional crafts were organized into large artisanal cooperatives (*sana'a*). These bodies were restricted to members of specialized clans, and the occupations were transmitted by hereditary right, membership being denied to any person who did not belong to the relevant caste. Status as a metalsmith, dyer, weaver, tanner, potter, butcher, or barber was handed down from father to son.[64]

Each caste was responsible for one of these occupations and provided professional training. The system survives, but today many occupations are not restricted, since new social conventions govern their practice in urban areas. On the margins of the traditional artisanry, more and more new occupations have emerged as a result of the introduction of new products and techniques from Europe; these can be practiced by anyone who has the requisite knowledge and a little capital. An examination of the *patentes* issued by the revenue service shows that occupations such as photographer and mechanic appeared during the 1960s; others such as metalworker or automobile electrician have developed even more recently, though one does find members of the metalsmiths' caste among the former.

Generally, these small activities are extremely diverse and respond quickly to the needs and preferences of the urban market. As a result, some occupations have become extinct: sellers of millet beer, who once were very numerous, have practically disappeared because the government has outlawed their activity; somewhat similarly, the establishment of Sonitan dealt a fatal blow to the tanners' association.

Growth in the Number of Small Producers

It is very hard to get precise statistics on small producers. The only government agency that collects annual data is the revenue service (which takes no account of activities that lack fixed infrastructure), as part of collecting fees for the *patentes*. Table 4.15, showing changes in the number of persons engaged in specific activities, testifies to the modern character of many occupations.

As mentioned earlier, microenterprises are essential to the town's absorption of immigrants; a study conducted in the Sabon Gari quarter shows that about 80 percent of recent arrivals (in Maradi less than five years) worked in such enterprises. The other 20 percent found work in the modern sector (government or industrial companies). The proliferation of small occupations is closely linked to the town's continuing demographic growth. Their

Table 4.15   Number of Workers in Certain Occupations

	1960	1966	1970	1975	1978	1980
Millet beer sellers	43	58	74	59	0	0
Photographers	0	2	5	9	10	12
Taxi drivers	0	0	0	0	42	94
Hairdressers/Barbers	7	7	10	16	13	14
Grain millers	8	8	19	27	30	36
Clock repairmen	0	0	1	3	3	3
Air conditioner repairmen	0	0	0	1	2	3
Tailors	78	44	106	94	84	118
Metalworkers	0	0	4	18	26	38

Source: General Revenue Service

number has multiplied rapidly, becoming a very important part of the city's economic life.

Principal Characteristics of Small Urban Operations

An earlier study covered five sectors of the informal economy, each with one or more occupations: clothing (tailors, shoemakers), construction (masons), small manufacturing (potters, metalsmiths, furniture makers), micro-commerce (table vendors, restaurateurs), transportation (taxi drivers).[65]

There were major differences among these activities. Those belonging to traditional crafts use simple techniques and are regulated by specific social rules (the caste system), while those of more recent origin use modern techniques and means of production (including machinery), and their work may be organized in ways that are similar to those of a small capitalist enterprise.

Despite the differences it is possible to identify some common characteristics, notably

- Levels of labor use
- Marketing problems
- Possibilities for accumulating capital
- Relations with officialdom

Labor is usually paid less than its value, and apprenticeship is a basic means of exploitation found in all sectors. It is a simple exchange of benefits: the patron agrees to train the apprentice in his occupation, in exchange for which the latter contributes his help more or less unpaid and obeys his master. Thus, a "moral" contract exists between patron and apprentice, linking them in a reciprocal relation. However, this relation differs from that described earlier with respect to commerce (the relationship of patron and servant—*uban-gida* and *bara*) to the extent that the master of the workshop contents himself to train his apprentice but does not later give him the material means to set himself up on his own, while the merchant eventually furnishes his dependent the means to start his own commerce.

In the traditional crafts, apprentices are often members of the workshop boss's family, their occupations still ruled by the caste system and transmitted by heredity. In more recent occupations, family connections between master and apprentice are not as important; there are even capitalistic relationships in some sectors (metalworkers), where one may encounter qualified workers who receive salaries.

Whatever the activity, the importance of apprenticeship is fundamental. It is thoroughly institutionalized in all sectors. The apprentices provide their masters an inexpensive labor pool; in return, they receive the minimum necessary to maintain their productive capacity (daily nourishment, lodging, pocket money) and thereby allow the workshop to maintain itself in a market where competition is very intense. To that extent, they appear to be prolonging the production characteristics of the traditional subsistence economy.

The principal characteristics of labor in the microeconomy are therefore as follows:

- The pay is low and usually in the form of gifts according to productivity.
- There is little in the way of formal salaries (except in activities similar to modern industry).
- Apprenticeships are very long: masters prolong the training period in order to avoid creating competitive producers in the market. They are expected to inculcate in apprentices not only the essential techniques but also the principles of a discipline to which the apprentices will submit for the rest of their professional lives.[66]
- Workers have no legal status and no organization to defend them.
- Work is seasonal (October until May) because of the rural origins of many workers, who return to their villages at the approach of the growing season in order to cultivate the fields.
- Future prospects are poor: the possibility of launching their own businesses appears utopian to many apprentices, who are overwhelmed by their social spending obligations (marriage, housing, etc.).

Producers face *marketing problems* in two directions: upstream in obtaining raw materials (except in certain cases such as pottery, where the materials can be found in nature) and downstream in selling their output.

The problems and irregular supply of raw materials in a town such as

Maradi constitute major preoccupations for many artisans, whose work may be disturbed or even stopped altogether. For example, the sites where masonry is under way may be shut down repeatedly for lack of cement. Even the furniture makers may have to stop work for lack of raw materials. The problems are more serious during the growing season (June until September) because the commercial offices are understaffed, many employees having left for the bush.

Nigeria's proximity, however, is an important asset. Many products essential to local artisans come from Kano. The prices for these goods fluctuate over the course of the year and are reflected in the costs of production. To that extent, artisans are subservient to market forces.

Commercial markets and distribution are likewise problems, since disposing of output is vital to every producer's survival. In accordance with their specialties, they may focus on supplying the public sector, city dwellers, merchants, or rural communities.[67] These markets are not mutually exclusive: furniture makers can work for ordinary citizens, merchants, and government all at the same time. Small manufacturing enterprises try hard to match the needs and desires of their clients; indeed, their adaptability and flexibility are a gauge of their likelihood of survival. Nevertheless, in order to serve the different markets just identified, they have to contend with two kinds of competition, external and internal.

External competition pits small urban producers against the modern sector, both local enterprises and imported manufactures. Sonitan and Fabmétal are among those local firms that compete directly with artisans. While the first succeeded in eliminating the traditional tanners, the second ultimately failed because it competed head-on with wood and metal furniture workers.

As for imports, the sale of foreign goods has forced several professions out of the market; for example, the arrival of plastic shoes in massive numbers disrupted the shoemakers, whose control over their raw material (leather) had previously forestalled any competition. Similarly, the weavers and the calabash sellers were hurt by imports of cloth and enamelware. The weavers now constitute a luxury craft whose products are aimed at a wealthy clientele (government employees and Europeans).

The competition with manufactured goods has had its greatest impact in mass consumption sectors, where industry can employ low-unit-cost production techniques. In such instances, the survival of the affected craft is far from certain.

Internal competition comes from producers within the same craft. It is strongest when there is an oversupply of producers in comparison with the size of distribution markets. Thus, it is accentuated by apprenticeships. As Charmes has noted, it is a general characteristic of the apprenticeship system that it creates new producers, including clandestine and amateur producers who intensify the competition.[68] This mainly affects prices, which are constrained to the maximum because of the low cost of labor. In many cases, the price of a good or service underrepresents its real value.

Wealth accumulation of the capitalist type involves the investment of part of the profits in order to grow capital and increase production. Examination of several sectors of activity (Table 4.16) shows that levels of profit (even assuming revenues are equivalent to profit) are insufficient to accumulate anything.[69] The average rates presented in Table 4.16 are based on samples from the units investigated in each sector. The lowest and highest limits are the margins in which most of the estimated revenues are found. The estimates are very likely close to reality; however, on one hand there are important gaps between productive units in the same sector, and on the other revenues are often random: an artisan might say, for example, "I didn't make any money at all for a week, but then I made a lot."

The revenue levels do not permit a regular process of saving. In the traditional occupations (pottery, smithing, shoemaking/leather working), they only allow workers to keep on working. In the more modern activities (wood and metal furniture making), artisans sometimes arrive at the point of saving capital, thereby moving from the stage of crafts to that of small enterprises.

Finally, the boss redistributes most revenues in accordance with family status; conversely, exceptional gains create occasions for close relatives to remind the fortunate one of his familial responsibilities.

Relations with government agencies are a reality in a town like Maradi, even though small urban enterprises are illegal if they are not officially registered and if applicable law, social law especially, is ignored. Broad intervention by the authorities into all these unsanctioned occupations is impossible, inasmuch as they are essential to the absorption of the unemployed and they produce essential goods and services for the population. Hence, the government limits its actions to combating fraud and illicit imports of Nigerian goods; this translates into seizures of stock from merchants and from the many table vendors.

Table 4.16   Monthly Revenues of Artisans, 1978 (in CFA francs)

Profession	Lower Limit	Higher Limit	Average Rate
Potters	10,000	25,000	19,000
Leather workers	5,000	15,000	13,000
Metalsmiths	8,000	25,000	17,000
Tailors	38,000	53,000	45,000
Carpenters	30,000	60,000	54,000
Masons	30,000	50,000	38,000
Restaurateurs	10,000	35,000	21,500
Table peddlers	10,000	35,000	16,000
Taxi drivers	40,000	90,000	55,000

Conclusion

In addition to the blossoming of its commerce, during the past few years Maradi experienced a diversification of its economy, illustrated in its energetic industrialization. During the recession under way in Niger in 1983–1984, industrialization experienced a series of failures. Nevertheless, perhaps there will be a recovery in the medium term, above all if the *Alhazai* decide to invest their capital increasingly in production, following a similar path to that of the merchants in northern Nigeria (whose hands may have been forced by disturbances in the import-export business).

Like other African cities, Maradi has an informal sector that plays an important role from the perspective of employment. Small urban economic activities allow the population to find the means to subsist. At Maradi, this sector has benefited from the side effects of commercial growth, which has stimulated the local economy. It has also benefited from proximity to Nigeria, which has made virtually every kind of trafficking possible.

NOTES

1. Niger thus lost its principal export product, uranium not yet having reached its later importance.
2. E. Grégoire, "Un système de production agro-pastoral en crise: le terroir de Gourjae (Niger)," in *Enjeux fonciers en Afrique noire* (Paris: Karthala, 1982).
3. Cowpeas are similar to black-eyed peas—Translator.
4. In keeping with the liberalization of the Nigerien economy, Sonara's monopoly of cowpeas was eliminated in 1983.
5. It rose from 10,000 metric tons in 1964 to 70,000 in 1979 in the *département* of Maradi alone.
6. The current low level of groundnut sales may also be due in part to the price gaps among official, parallel, and Nigerian markets. It appears that part of production escapes Sonara's grasp and is sold to merchants who resell it on traditional markets or have it processed, whereupon it is resold by market vendors.
7. As noted earlier, the public sector has been growing at the expense of private business since the end of the 1960s.
8. They had a bit invested in other sectors (construction, transport), but not enough to limit the risks.
9. Unfortunately, this situation was strikingly illustrated during the rainy season of 1984, which saw a very large rainfall deficit. The government of Niger was forced to appeal for international help to cover the harvest shortfall and to avoid a new famine.
10. The producer price for millet was 13 CFA francs in 1949 and 12.5 CFA francs in 1971.
11. Cereals merchants specializing in millet seldom deal in any other commodities.
12. *Annuaire économique du Niger,* 1973–1974.
13. The pattern of variations in price during the course of the year is identical to that described for groundnuts during the colonial period. Farmers who

do not have a pressing need for money can always get a better price for their crops if they wait to sell.

14. OPVN was buying millet from the farmers at 8,000 CFA francs a bag. As soon as the official marketing campaign ended, the price fell because of the oversupply, and the merchants bought at 4,500 CFA francs a bag, reselling it for double that amount.

15. Decree No. 82-64/PCMS/MFP/T of April 29, 1982, allows civil servants to devote every Saturday to producing grain for their own consumption. The decision created some difficulties with land use on the outskirts of towns.

16. Raynaut, "Le cas de la région de Maradi."

17. The trucker *Alhaji* Boubakar, whose life is sketched in Chapter 3, owns a large orchard at the gates of town.

18. I. Bagayogo, "Emergence d'une bourgeoisie agraire au Mali: exemple des planteurs de la région de Bamako," doctoral thesis, third cycle, Ecole des Hautes Etudes en Sciences Sociales, 1982.

19. The nomads traveled to Maradi in the hope of finding help and livestock feed there. Their numbers were estimated at 38,000 in 1973–1974, distributed among sixty camps. On this subject, see P. Sawadogo, "Enquête sur les nomades refoulés par la sécheresse, zones de Maradi et Dakoro, Niger" (Dakar: Training for the Environment Program, IDEP-UNEP-SIDA, 1974).

20. The herd was devastated anew by drought in 1984. It appears that in order to avoid repeating the losses experienced in 1973, the herders sold animals in massive numbers but at very low prices.

21. Many senior officials of the civilian government invested their money in livestock, which they placed in the care of Peul herders. See Guy Nicolas, "Remarques sur divers facteurs socio-économiques de la famine au sein d'une société subsaharienne," in *Drought in Africa* (London: International African Institute, 1977), pp. 159–169.

22. According to several sources, the Maradi nobility were very active in the livestock business at the time, and the provincial chief himself owned a sizable herd of cattle.

23. The most important livestock trader in Maradi owned a herd of more than 1,000 head of cattle and was one of the richest of the *Alhazai*.

24. M. Sar, "Louga: la ville et sa région," doctoral thesis, third cycle, University of Dakar.

25. The Development Society was somewhat analogous to a political party—Translator.

26. As with Sonara, the new Copro-Niger raised African firms to the same level as European firms.

27. His name has been changed here.

28. It should be noted that *Alhaji* Moussa had not been involved in the groundnut trade.

29. Source: Copro-Niger, Maradi.

30. Raynaut, "Le cas de la région de Maradi."

31. Cloth transshipments began around 1974. The Nigerians built a textile mill in western Nigeria to imitate Dutch fabrics, which led to protectionist measures limiting cloth imports. However, the quality was inferior and there was not enough to meet demand. As a result, the protectionist measures were subverted, using the existing system that operated via Maradi.

32. The retail stores were closed in 1983, apparently as a result of lobbying from private merchants, who complained about the competition.

33. Dominique Rega, "Les sociétés commerciales françaises en Afrique, ou les tribulations d'un impérialisme mercantile," in *La France contre l'Afrique*,

a special issue of *Tricontinental* (Paris: Maspéro, 1981), pp. 172–182.

34. The names of these businessmen have been altered.

35. *Alhazai* who had been active in politics devoted themselves solely to business after the 1974 coup d'état.

36. P. Hill, "Notes on the History of the Northern Katsina Tobacco Trade," in *Studies in Rural Capitalism in West Africa*, African Studies Series 2 (Cambridge: Cambridge University Press, 1970).

37. If the goods exceed the time limit, the Nigerien customs agents impose a penalty tax of 2.5 percent of their value.

38. Such a study would be fascinating and would have to be carried out on both sides of the frontier. However, it would require considerable material resources as well as strong governmental support (including authorization to do research in Nigeria).

39. In theory, a simple license suffices. In practice, transit trade requires very large amounts of money (in addition, the banks now lend less willingly than before), which is why the number of merchants trading with Nitra is so limited.

40. Transit trade financing is one of the principal activities of the banks (BDRN and BIAO).

41. The borders remained closed from April 1984 until March 1986, at which point the Federal Republic of Nigeria, advised by representatives of the World Bank, adopted a sweeping program of economic and financial policy reform. As noted above, the closing impeded transit traffic only marginally while it remained in force, and afterwards the pattern of trade in cigarettes and other illicit goods resumed as before—Translator.

42. From "Plan de transports," a transportation study conducted by the Bureau de Contrôle et d'Etudes d'Outre-Mer for the government of Niger. In contrast to the tonnage deficit, trade provides the Maradi region a very large net surplus when it is measured by value. For example, during fourth quarter 1977, imports from Nigeria were worth 72.6 million CFA francs, while transit exports were valued at 3.3 billion CFA francs.

43. Smuggling of cowpeas is now widespread: bought at 45 CFA francs per kilogram by Sonara and at 75 CFA francs by private merchants, cowpeas are selling in Nigeria for the equivalent of 120 to 130 CFA francs per kilogram.

44. This activity has put certain "money changers" on easy street. Some sit boldly just outside the doors to the banks, while others travel back and forth continually between Maradi and Kano.

45. Nicolas, "La pratique traditionelle du crédit."

46. The speculation links players in Kano, London, New York, and Maradi.

47. Nigeria's recent economic difficulties have driven down the value of the naira. In April 1983 it was worth about 200 CFA francs, then fell to 145 CFA francs in March 1984, and by August 1984 had reached 100 CFA francs.

48. The Europeans did not always sell to Africans under good conditions, especially after the 1974 coup d'état, when many of them quickly sold off their assets for fear of nationalizations that never took place.

49. The decline in the total number of buildings constructed and of *patentes* paid in 1976, and also the sharp increases recorded in 1983, are due to changes in the tax rates.

50. It also allowed food and livestock traders to make very profitable deals.

51. Sawadogo, "Enquête sur les nomades refoulés par la sécheresse."

52. The project, financed by the World Bank (at 1 billion CFA francs per year), has provided the town many benefits by creating jobs and by offering opportunities for work to artisans and small enterprises.

53. Bureau de Contrôle et d'Etudes d'Outre-Mer, "Plan de transports."

54. It is said that one *Alhaji* set up a parallel market bank whose principal operations were lending and foreign exchange. Given the clandestine nature of this institution, it was impossible to obtain precise information about it.

55. Among the *Alhazai* who took part in both types of commerce (groundnuts as well as manufactured products) with the European firms, many were forced to abandon the second when Sonara was created. The firms advanced credit that the merchants could repay from groundnut commissions and profits. As soon as the European firms lost their monopolies and found themselves on the same footing as the African merchants, they reorganized, keeping only those merchants whom they deemed serious and creditworthy. (In any case, they advanced very little credit from then on.)

56. Uranium metal production grew as follows: 410.5 metric tons in 1971, 867 in 1972, 1,116.9 in 1974, 1,461.9 in 1976, 2,061 in 1978, and 4,200 in 1981. The price rose from 5,400 CFA francs per kilogram in 1974 to 24,000 CFA francs in 1979 but then fell to 20,000 CFA francs in 1981.

57. A study of competition between this firm and the artisanal shops is reported in Emmanuel Grégoire, "Les perspectives d'accumulation dans la petite industrie de transformation: l'exemple de la menuiserie métallique à Maradi (Niger)," in *Villes africaines au microscope*, a special issue of *Cahiers d'Etudes Africaines*, 21, 1-3 (1981–1983).

58. His name has been changed.

59. The *Alhazai* often choose jobbers who will work for very low wages.

60. This tendency is reflected in the number of licenses (595 in 1980, 185 in 1979) recorded by the Labor Department in the modern sector of the economy comprising industry, construction, and public works.

61. It is noteworthy that Sonipal was created using private capital only; a single *Alhaji* provided 80 percent.

62. The government, and for that matter the Maradi rural development project financed by the World Bank, employs more people than the entire industrial sector (600 at any given moment for the project alone).

63. Philippe Hugon, "Les petites activités marchandes dans les espaces urbains africains: essai de typologie," *Revue Tiers-Monde*, No. 82, Vol. 21, April-June 1980.

64. Barbers played an important role in baptismal and circumcision ceremonies.

65. Emmanuel Grégoire, "L'artisanat dans la ville de Maradi" (Republic of Niger: Ministry of Plan, Service Départemental, 1979).

66. These conditions recall those of apprenticeship in France during the seventeenth and eighteenth centuries, when the apprentice was also totally dependent upon the master until he became a qualified worker and assumed his full rights in the enterprise. While in certain professions there was no fee for apprenticeship, as in Africa, in others (glaziers, etc.) the apprentice was expected to pay the master a certain sum that was in some sense an entrance fee into the profession and a payment for the training. Cf. *Histoire Economique et Sociale de la France*, Vol. 2 (Paris: Presses Universitaires de France, 1970).

67. The different government agencies and in particular the city administration and the Maradi rural development project have often called for bids from artisans and small entrepreneurs in recent years. These institutions have done their share to invigorate and develop the small business sector.

68. J. Charmes, "Les contradictions du développement du secteur non structuré," in *Secteur informel et petite production marchande dans les villes du Tiers-Monde*, in *Revue Tiers-Monde*, No. 82, Vol. 21, April-June 1980.

69. Grégoire, "L'artisanat dans la ville de Maradi."

5

The Social Content
of Maradi's Evolution

The political and economic history of Maradi demonstrates the important changes it has undergone in recent decades. The capital of a clearly delineated Hausa warrior chiefdom in the nineteenth century, Maradi became an administrative headquarters and a trading center during the colonial period. After the independence of Niger, its growth accelerated; in twenty years it was transformed from a large town to a small city, expanding vigorously. This rise, due initially to groundnut exports and later to commercial exchanges with Nigeria, allowed Maradi to become a veritable economic dynamo stimulating the surrounding region.

The rapid growth had a social consequence. The town has produced a variety of new social groups, among them a commercial and bureaucratic bourgeoisie and a multitude of workers—artisans, laborers, small merchants, and others.

The interjection of Maradi into a vast economic space characterized by the globalization of its exchanges prompted the emergence of a merchant capitalism symbolized by the *Alhazai*. It was the town itself that allowed them to flourish, just as it allowed the appearance of a vast crowd of workers who survive from day to day solely by the fruit of their own labor.

As history attests, such social cleavages are usually produced in cities because cities constitute a kind of prophetic environment. They are better suited than the rural world to anticipate social evolution, better able to sketch out what lies in the future. Thus, it is worthwhile to describe several of the mutations that local society has undergone and to identify some of the new social actors who have taken their places on Maradi's stage.

FORMATION OF A BOURGEOISIE

Defining the notion of a bourgeoisie is a delicate task, for the term can take on various meanings according to time and place. It would be difficult to define any social group and apply uniform criteria to it without taking into account the economic milieu in which it exists. If by chance the fortunate class recently emerging in Africa's urban societies presents striking resemblances to others, for example to the French commercial bourgeoisie of the seventeenth and eighteenth centuries, it nonetheless displays important differences and characteristics of its own.

Thus, rather than attempt to define what is meant by bourgeoisie with respect to this group, it would be preferable first to describe some of its traits: its mode of ascension, its economic and social objectives, and the strategies it employs in order to achieve them. This makes it easier to appreciate its originality.

The Rise of a Local Bourgeoisie

The *Alhazai* achieved success in three stages:

1. At the end of the nineteenth century and the beginning of the twentieth, Maradi provided merchants only a limited scope for commercial activity: they could mount a few expeditions toward the south (to Kano or perhaps farther away), returning with cloth and cola nuts exchanged for livestock, hides, and skins. These expeditions were the principal activity of the *madougou* who led the convoys.

2. The peace imposed by colonial rule and the establishment of a trade economy brought about the appearance of new merchants acting as intermediaries between the European commercial houses and local producers and consumers. This first group of *Alhazai*, closely linked to the Europeans and to their companies, profited from the intensification of the trade economy after 1945: the growth of groundnut production and transport, the deepening penetration of manufactured goods, and the creation of modern infrastructure all stimulated their activities.

After independence, the government of Niger facilitated their efforts; it helped the *Alhazai* to reach a level of equality with the European firms and at times to take advantage of the Europeans' retreat from various sectors of activity. However, these particular *Alhazai*, tightly integrated into the trade economy as they were, were unable to adapt to changing market conditions at the end of the 1960s.

3. From 1967 on, certainly in the course of the 1970s, the earlier constraints on local commerce were invalidated by a series of coincidental events (war in Biafra, drought, increased government earnings from uranium)

and structural changes (creation of institutions with mixed state and private ownership).

These changes encouraged the emergence of a new generation of merchants who were much more modern and enterprising than their predecessors, *Alhazai* who invested in a multiplicity of domains (real estate, transportation, industry, etc.), used modern banking (notably to obtain credit), created commercial networks extending far beyond the local region, nurtured links with the large-scale merchants in Kano, and established ties with powerful politicians. For example, some *Alhazai* became active in the PPN/RDA political party, and many of them later participated in the Samaria movement and in the new national political party of Niger, the Société de Développement.[1] These relations with the political milieu are not always disinterested, since the wealth of many *Alhazai* relies upon political support. (This was especially true during the regime of President Diori Hamani, but it has not disappeared.)

The forming of this new generation of *Alhazai* marks an important division within the merchant class, which is becoming more differentiated. It is worth noting that this class remains open and is not obligated to any particular group in the local social structure: anyone with initiative, luck, and a good sponsor can become wealthy. The relationship between patron and client (described in Chapter 3) remains essential; entry into the clientele of a major merchant, a dispenser of large favors, constitutes a trump card for getting ahead in the world of business and in the social hierarchy.

This elective relationship, which reinforces the relationship of lineage, is one of the key elements of Hausa social structure; it explains the success of many merchants. For example, an *Alhaji* who had worked for the government entered the service of a major merchant in Maradi during the mid-1970s. After several years he then became a representative for a rich merchant in Niamey. Although he remained the dependent (*bara*) of someone more powerful than he, this *Alhaji* developed his own business, and today he is a personage whose fortune is widely respected.[2]

Before we examine the purposes of this merchant group, we must examine a key element in its ascension: access to credit. The biographies of the *Alhazai* demonstrate that all of those who have enjoyed success have had ready access to credit. If the European companies in their time allowed certain men to accumulate wealth quickly, the banks (in particular BDRN) took up the cause after independence; they not only supported but also actively promoted local commerce. Without the powerful structure of credit, the efflorescence of Maradi's great merchants would not have been possible.

During the 1980s the banks lent money more parsimoniously (interest rates were 18.5 percent in 1982) because of the bankruptcy of numerous merchants. As a result, the more fortunate *Alhazai* now guarantee with their own assets the loans contracted by others, the provincial chief being one of the principal guarantors. They earn some interest, but more importantly they gain prestige, for in the Hausa culture, possession of wealth has value only to the extent it is well known. It is better to be surrounded by many dependents and debtors than to have capital immobilized. A wealthy person thus finds it difficult to refuse to lend money or refuse to guarantee a bank loan.

The Objectives of the Local Bourgeoisie

The principal objective of the *Alhazai* is to solidify and extend their commercial position. The accumulation of wealth, whether in goods or capital, motivates much of their activity. However, this is not their sole objective, inasmuch as Hausa society considers that an individual has no economic weight unless he has a social weight, a "richness in men" (*arzikin mutane*).

Wealth in Goods and Capital

A merchant defines himself as someone who can make a profit on virtually any endeavor. Although big business may absorb much of their attention, merchants will not pass up an opportunity to participate in some petty speculation that might produce a nice return.[3] The richest *Alhazai* are those who have escaped from specialization into diversity; they show a disposition and an aptitude to seize every opportunity to make money. This diversification, however, does not exclude favoring one category of activity or another; for example, the activities of *Alhaji* Number Two (see Figure 4.5) concentrate on the transit trade. Nonetheless, he also deals in manufactured goods, participates in capitalizing various companies, invests in real estate, and so on.

Although these are profitable opportunities, it is noteworthy that the notion of profit is not the result of a written difference between revenues and expenses.[4] The *Alhazai*'s gains are therefore very difficult to evaluate. The task is made even more arduous by the confidential nature of many operations; even the local bankers do not know about certain transactions.[5]

Nevertheless, despite the absence of a clearly defined concept of profit, the process of capital accumulation, once begun, has expanded. It occurs in many ways, one of the most common being investment in real estate. The banks have stimulated this by demanding stronger and stronger collateral (property deeds, stock certificates) in order to cover their loans; this pushes the *Alhazai* to invest in real property, since access to credit is essential for many commercial transactions.

During the 1970s and 1980s, investment gradually extended to landholding: the establishment of orchards and large farms was certainly not a new phenomenon, but the drought certainly encouraged it. Agriculture became a profit-making economic activity.

Most *Alhazai* judge industrial investment to be risky and relatively less profitable. During an interview, one of them explained: "I make a lot of money from commerce. If I build a factory, I will earn a lower rate of return and I will have problems with both the managers and the workers, who will steal my goods." This seems to be the attitude of many *Alhazai*, even those who have invested capital in companies. They have been led to invest more by a desire for a good image as "contributing to the country's development" than by any hope of profits. Under the circumstances, industrial growth remains the responsibility of the Nigerien government.

Capitalism therefore remains linked to commerce; it has not yet made the transition to industrial capitalism of the kind developed in Europe during the nineteenth century. The transformation has not yet occurred in Niger even though it began in Nigeria as early as the 1970s, when wealthy African investors began participating in the industrialization of the country. Some *Alhazai* very ably invested part of their wealth in Nigeria (at Katsina and Kano, for example), perhaps trying to protect themselves against possibly unfavorable future political changes in Niger.

Arzikin Mutane

The accumulation of goods or capital is not the only objective of the *Alhazai*. Richness in men is basic; in Hausa society, it helps to confirm economic status. The behavior of important people (nobles, rich merchants) often focuses on surface appearances, even ostentation. As a result, they spend large sums and give away part of their wealth for reasons of prestige.

The *Alhazai* conform to this custom, their economic success manifesting itself in a variety of ways. Most have several wives, since Islam allows a man to have up to four.[6] As a result, they have many children; one man has been heard to complain that his family responsibilities are too heavy, as he has twenty-nine children. The *Alhazai*'s homes are also symbols: the richest own imposing one-story houses of modern materials provided with every comfort (air conditioning, television, videocassette players, refrigerators, freezers, etc.). Finally, their vehicles are, as in Europe, external signs of wealth; the richest *Alhazai*, who drive shiny Mercedes cars, all rush to buy the new models as soon as they come out.

Aside from this material wealth, the *Alhazai* display their success through the distribution of many gifts to those around them, surrounding themselves with retinues rivaling that of the provincial chief. They strive to extend their ascendancy over as many people as possible, to increase what the Hausa language calls, in a telling phrase, a fortune in men (*arzikin mutane*). This notion remains important even in an urbanizing culture such as that of Maradi; the economic worth of an individual remains closely linked to social worth. Merchants thus need a large number of people to maintain and extend their commercial networks. Therefore, merchants must distribute a portion of their wealth, especially among those members of their networks who are the basis of their economic strength.

These networks rest in large part upon a relation between patron (*ubangida*) and servant (*bara*). Raynaut notes that

> this interpersonal rapport—which exceeds that of master and servant—exists from the moment a state of inferiority and availability in one party, and of superiority and authority in the other, is created between two people. As soon as a man is linked with another by his obligations, he becomes his *bara*. Still, although the relationship is asymmetrical, there is no less a reciprocity, for when the *bara* places himself at the disposition of his *ubangida*, it is in exchange for the protection the latter provides. It is the dependence of the first that in itself constitutes a counterpart to the gifts and the assistance provided by the second.[7]

The dependents (*barori*) are the first to receive favors (*alheri*) from the *Alhazai*, and the number of dependents provides one measure of an *Alhaji*'s actual commercial network. The *Alhazai* also give away part of their wealth in the form of gifts and assistance (*saddaka*) to the poor, the sick, and those down on their luck (*arziki*). For example, one *Alhaji* paid to have the metalworking shops in Maradi build wheelchairs for the crippled.

Michel Agier correctly notes that *alheri* implies a client relationship and, in a sense, constitutes a remuneration extended by a merchant to one of his dependents (*bara*). *Saddaka*, by contrast, is charity given without compensation. In any case, the acts have a character of ostentation, falling under the rubric of competition and rivalry among rich *Alhazai*. Any means whatever is acceptable for advertising their great generosity.[8] They will do anything to show their wealth and build up their prestige among the people.[9]

In addition to presents offered to their dependents or to the needy, the *Alhazai* give services to the government, especially in the areas of public health and city administration.[10] One *Alhaji* paid for the construction of a dispensary dedicated in his name; another provided a number of ambulances, each emblazoned with a sign informing everyone of his gift; a third bought a number of garbage trucks. These acts allow them not only to demonstrate their generosity but also to obtain favors from government agencies.

These points emphasize that the *Alhazai*'s behavior is not motivated solely by profit; they are still influenced by considerations of social status. The importance of appearances remains at the center of their concerns. It is without a doubt a motive greater than their "generosity" or their altruism. Moreover, it is worth considering that some *Alhazai* find themselves in something of a potlatch situation in which each gift by an *Alhaji* constitutes a challenge to the others to make a gift of equal if not superior value. The situation may disturb some of them, who would prefer to invest their capital in more productive ways, but they are obliged to submit one way or another in order to protect their reputations.

These rivalries among rich *Alhazai* are also revealed in the area of religion: if the *Alhazai* do not have a profound knowledge of the Quran, as do the merchant members of Muslim sects in Senegal, for example, nonetheless they demonstrate their faith—and their wealth—by financing the construction of mosques. In town, they build small mosques in various neighborhoods. In the bush, especially in the administrative centers for *arrondissements* where there may not yet be a major mosque, they build edifices whose cost may surpass several hundred million CFA francs. For example, the trucker *Alhaji* Boubakar is now financing the construction of a large mosque at Tessaoua.

Executing Social Strategies

How do the major merchants achieve their economic and social objectives? Within the merchant bourgeoisie, there are several types of economic and social strategies. Before describing them in detail, I offer the following classifications of economic operators and their strategies.

Types of Merchants

The task is not easy, since the commercial processes described do not fit neatly into a rigid framework. However, it is possible to define several broad categories according to one of the most important measures, namely, level of activity. Differing strategies can be rather clearly identified on the basis of this distinction.

The nature of the business and the degree of its diversification might also provide useful categories, yet these turn out to be less useful than a system that classifies according to the size of the business. The latter comprises three main categories:

1. As of the mid-1980s there existed a very small group of individuals (four in all) whose level of business clearly separated them from all others. Their annual revenues are impossible to evaluate precisely, given not only their secretiveness but also the diversity of their operations. However, their annual turnover was at least 2 billion CFA francs, probably more (between 5 billion and perhaps 7 to 8 billion CFA francs).[11] The profits from this volume of business, certainly the profits from the transit business, were on the order of 6 percent of revenues. This level of success and the wealth it engendered were of very recent origin, dating to the beginning of the Biafran war in 1967. They were due primarily to the growth of the transit trade between Maradi and Nigeria.

2. The middle group of merchants had more members (about fifteen), but their level of activity was more modest. They were in an income group whose lower limit was about 200 million CFA francs, and whose upper limit (in exceptional cases) approached 2 billion CFA francs. As is the case with the first group, success was largely due to transit trade with Nigeria.

However, several merchants (truckers and those dealing in livestock) appear to have profited specifically from the drought, while others took advantage of the government's spending programs following the increase in fiscal revenues generated by uranium exports.

3. The lowest group contains the most members, some forty to fifty individuals. Their revenues totaled 50 million to 100 million CFA francs a year. Compared to the two preceding groups, they achieved their success more gradually; in some cases their businesses dated back to the colonial period. The group included some former groundnut traders as well as merchants dealing in traditional goods such as cola nuts or livestock.

The foregoing typology is deliberately approximate because of the problem of obtaining information about the level of revenues and the number of members in each group; nevertheless, it does focus attention on the relative economic power of various *Alhazai*, which in turn helps clarify their economic strategies.

Economic Strategies

The *richest* group was distinctive because of its small size, only four members. Two of them, already described in Figure 8, achieved enormous diversity; they went well beyond specialization, becoming involved in all kinds of transactions and displaying a remarkable aptitude and capacity to find and exploit every available opportunity for profit. This strategy helped them to limit risk, since a loss from one kind of deal could be offset by gains from others.

Another of their characteristics was geographic dispersion. Although they made their headquarters at Maradi, their operations extended to Niamey and to Kano and other major Nigerian cities. They had contacts in other African countries, Benin and Togo in particular, and even in countries on other continents, notably for the transit trade: France, Great Britain, the United States, Japan. They often traveled to these countries themselves, or they sent dependents (*barori*) as their representatives.[12]

The credit banks extended to them was essential for their transit business. It was easy for them to obtain credit given the extent of their assets, which included real estate in Maradi, Niamey, Zinder, and Nigeria, as well as trucks and other transportation equipment. Investment in industrial production did not interest them much, and the sums they invested were negligible compared to their total revenues.

At the time, these four *Alhazai* figured among the most important entrepreneurs in Niger. Their business strategy can best be demonstrated by tracing their business biographies. The example given below faithfully illustrates the method of wealth accumulation employed by the other three.

Alhaji Habou entered commerce with one of his brothers at a very early age.[13] He went to Kano with him to sell hides, returning to Maradi with cola nuts that they sold at wholesale and retail. Upon the death of his brother, at the beginning of the 1940s, *Alhaji* Habou launched a fabric shop in partnership with a friend, who would buy in Djibya or Katsina (Nigeria) while he remained in Maradi to sell. The business lasted four or five years, after which he went on his own, buying small quantities of cloth from CFAO, which kept extensive stocks in the years following the war. The business gradually prospered, with merchants from towns such as Tessaoua or villages in the bush coming in often to buy percales or cretonnes; they knew *Alhaji* Habou would have a regular supply, for he had gained the confidence of a European, the chief buyer at CFAO, who would advance him merchandise on credit.

In addition to his regular clients, *Alhaji* Habou had agents in the city streets and in the nearby villages. Gradually, thanks to his organizing skills, he became one of the principal merchants in Maradi. The Nigerians began to buy fabric from him, and in 1967 their purchases increased substantially because the Biafran war disrupted supply lines within Nigeria. *Alhaji* Habou took advantage of the opportunity and his business thrived. As a result, in 1969 the reorganized Copro-Niger chose him as one of its certified dealers.

From then on he had access to bank credit, BDRN often providing funds for his transactions with Copro-Niger and with European firms. He bought wholesale (cloth, sugar, tea, etc.) under Copro-Niger's import monopoly and either distributed to other merchants who were not certified or sold at retail through his dependent agents. By 1971 *Alhaji* Habou, along with the other three major *Alhazai*, controlled a substantial portion of the market for Copro-Niger's monopoly imports. This put him in a privileged position to exploit the transit trade in cigarettes and fabrics as it developed during the early 1970s.

His operations became more and more diverse, and he turned increasingly toward Nigeria. Although he continued to wholesale manufactured goods imported by Copro-Niger and the Europeans, he concentrated on transit trade, enjoying active support from the banks. He and the other three major *Alhazai* in Maradi were among the very few who could always deliver cigarettes to the dealers in Kano. The profits were enormous.

Beginning in 1974, he began to reinvest his gains in real estate. He bought the location of one of the large European houses. He built villas. Extending his reach further, he controlled a significant part of the foreign exchange business involving naira and CFA francs.[14]

He continued in the transit trade after Copro-Niger abandoned it in 1975 but remained one of the company's main wholesalers as late as 1980. Because his commercial networks were extensive and well managed, he could move merchandise in the city and in the bush with equal ease. In 1982 he formed a partnership with three other dealers to import and distribute cereal grains.

This man's example clearly demonstrates the path to success followed by the other three major *Alhazai*. Their strategy consisted of gradual diversification of operations and geographic extension of the market served. For each of the four, the creation of Copro-Niger and the expansion of the transit trade were the key determinants of their successful accumulation of great wealth; thus, their recent and rapid progress was a product of the 1970s. None of the four participated in the groundnut collection business, which tends to confirm the proposition that trade in manufactured goods was more profitable than trade in groundnuts. They also had no difficulty in rebuilding their business after the drought.

The fifteen merchants in the *middle* category generated less business individually, but they also pursued more varied strategies. As in the preceding case, increasing volume tended to mean increasing diversification. Nevertheless, not every member of the group pursued the diversification strategy; several remained specialists in a single activity, such as transportation or livestock sales. The group's operations focused almost entirely on commerce; they left industrial production alone. Their geographic range was also more restricted; they did business mainly in Niger and Nigeria and perhaps in other African countries but rarely on any other continent.

They had less access to modern credit because the banks scrutinized their loan applications with greater care. In the case of BDRN, if the loan requested exceeded 30 million CFA francs, the file was transmitted to the head office at Niamey. According to information provided by the banks, some members of the middle group were in delicate to poor financial health, such that they had to mortgage their property. Their business, insufficiently diversified, was threatened by the hazards of the economic downturn.

Regardless of the timing or type of their operations, their success and their strategies were fairly heterogenous; however, three major patterns can be distinguished:

1. Several used methods similar to those of *Alhaji* Habou, albeit without achieving his volume. Between 1969 and 1971, following the restructuring of commerce, their operations were not large enough for them to be designated one of Copro-Niger's seven wholesalers. As a result, they found themselves in subordinate roles, whether selling manufactures or engaging in the transit trade. In 1972 they became Copro-Niger wholesalers, able to obtain products directly without any intermediary between themselves and the firm. This was not the case with regard to transit trade; most continued to be subcontractors to the four major *Alhazai*. In their case, the strategy of diversification was manifested through investment in real estate in order to gain readier access to bank credit.

2. For the others, success came about because of one *conjoncture* (series of critical coincidences) or another: drought, changes in exchange rates, or perhaps political favoritism created circumstances where wealth

accumulated rapidly. Several merchants became rich very quickly at the beginning of the 1970s, although their earlier operations had been quite modest. From that point they diversified, but they were unable to catch up with the richest four.

3. In a third set of cases success came very slowly, with very little diversification. The example of *Alhaji* Boubakar, cited earlier, is one such case, as is that of *Alhaji* Oumarou, a Maradi entrepreneur.[15] Born in a village near Maradi, *Alhaji* Oumarou worked from the age of ten years for a woman, *Hadjia* Hawa, who dealt in fabrics between Djibya and Kano, in Nigeria, and Maradi.[16] During the day, he would traverse the city streets selling goods she provided him each morning. In exchange, she fed him and offered him gifts. After living like this for many years, *Alhaji* Oumarou returned to his native village to be married. Some time later he returned to Maradi and went into business for himself, for *Hadjia* Hawa had abandoned her earlier business in order to sell cooked food.

His first effort involved cola nuts, but he lacked the specialized knowledge required, so he abandoned it and returned to selling fabrics. About 1968 he observed that the construction business was growing and that CFAO had the market to itself. He opened a lumber yard in Sabon Gari, quickly expanding to include cement, tiles, plumbing fixtures, and other construction materials. As all these items came from Nigeria, *Alhaji* Oumarou had to obtain import licenses. His business prospered, allowing him to open a second and then a third outlet.

In 1974 he got the idea of starting a construction firm. He hired several technically qualified workers and a bookkeeper. At about that time the government of Niger, whose resources were increasing, launched a number of construction projects in the town, including schools and dispensaries. Several of these projects were awarded to *Alhaji* Oumarou. Because his means were still quite modest, he frequently had to subcontract parts of his projects to other firms, despite his having recently bought a company belonging to a European.

By the mid-1980s *Alhaji* Oumarou figured among the principal businessmen in Maradi. The creation of his own company was the decisive step on his path to wealth. Like the trucker *Alhaji* Boubakar, he diversified his operations very little; aside from his construction business, he had a large plot of farmland on the outskirts of Maradi, owned some livestock, invested in real property, and dabbled in one form of trade or another as opportunity presented itself. As his experience shows, the second group offered greater variety of situation and strategy than the first, and the methods and time frame of wealth accumulation were noticeably different.

The *final* group comprises about fifty individuals who received the least revenues (between 50 million and 200 million CFA francs a year) and achieved the least diversity in their operations. Some engaged in only one or two lines of business, specializing, for example, in livestock, millet, cola nuts, or manufactures. They concentrated on internal markets in Niger and on the region around Maradi especially; they frequented the major markets at Maradi, Tessaoua, Dakoro, and other towns. Notwithstanding these limits, specialists in certain lines such as livestock, beans, and cola nuts did maintain contacts with merchants in other African countries, Nigeria in particular.

Their various assets, such as property titles, were not always sufficient to give them access to bank credit. As a result, at times one of the richer *Alhazai* would guarantee their borrowings. Some appeared to be dependents or fronts for wealthier entrepreneurs, who used them to disguise a portion of their activities. This practice is frequent in Hausa commercial circles; it sometimes happens that a millionaire (in CFA francs) *Alhaji* turns out to be acting for someone more important than he.

The rise of these men was usually gradual, in contrast to the rapid successes observed in the other two groups. For some, entry into personal dependency with respect to a more important merchant was the determining factor in allowing them to obtain credit and to develop their own businesses. For others, wealth came as the result of long, laborious effort in one business. Also, the former groundnut traders and *organismes-stockeurs* figured among this third group; these were entrepreneurs who reached the apogee of their careers during the 1950s and 1960s. Like *Alhaji* Ousmane, many stagnated at a modest level of activity: having abandoned the collecting of groundnuts, they turned to other trade as opportunities presented themselves. Others, such as *Alhaji* Maman, were quite successful in making a transition.[17]

Alhaji Maman is an influential member of the Maradi nobility. For a few years when very young he was a tailor's apprentice with a highly regarded tailor and dressmaker in town, *Alhaji* Alasanne, to whom he is related. He quickly abandoned this craft in favor of the fabric trade, which he judged to be more profitable. He bought at wholesale from the import houses and resold in places such as Guidan-Roumji, Madaoua, Dogaraoua, and Galmi. The latter towns being in the area where onions are grown, he bought large quantities of onions to sell upon his return to Maradi.

As his business prospered, *Alhaji* Maman decided to go into groundnut buying, making his first purchases for the Levantine trader Elias Issa, and later for *Alhaji* Daouda, then the principal Nigerien *organisme-stockeur*, with whom he worked for some ten years. When the groundnut trade declined, he shifted to trading in millet, which he bought in Nigeria for sale in Niger. With the end of the groundnut trade, not willing to depend only on millet, he sought other revenue sources, becoming one of Copro-Niger's certified wholesalers in 1974. He was thus able to obtain merchandise that he could resell as wholesaler, distributor, and retailer, thanks to his network of dependents.

In addition, he realized that if trade in cereal grains were profitable in the aftermath of the drought, millet production would be even more so. Probably because of his position in the nobility, he already owned numerous fields around Maradi, so he began both rain-fed grain production and market gardening. To promote his business, he went in with another merchant to obtain government import licenses for cereal grains, supplying the mining towns in northern Niger.

Following the confrontation between the government and the merchants concerning millet marketing (see the first section of Chapter 4), the cereals business was less lucrative, so *Alhaji* Maman turned to the transit trade, doing a bit of business in close association with Maradi's grandest *Alhazai*. To round out his activities, he also invested in real estate, no doubt to facilitate obtaining bank credit, and he speculated a bit in the foreign exchange market.

Conclusion

The foregoing typology of wealth among the *Alhazai* highlights the degree of diversity with regard to volume of business and economic strategy (Table 5.1). It reveals a rough correlation between business volume and two other factors—diversity of activities and geographic scope of operations.

Despite the differences among members, the *Alhazai* constitute a social group, distinguishable by wealth and lifestyle, that finds unity in its ideology and its place in local society. The development of such a class at Maradi has very likely been duplicated in other African urban communities. In addition, it offers some parallels with the economic and social history of France.

In the fifteenth century, French merchants did not figure among the great merchant princes of Europe, who were then mostly Italian and Flemish; for various reasons, they lagged behind. Foreigners dominated the market for quality fabrics, spices, and metal products. French merchants often served as agents for foreigners, and their activity was often limited to the distribution of imports within the French realm and the concentration of French merchandise for export.[18]

In contact with these foreigners, French merchants of Lyon, Paris, Bordeaux, and other large cities were initiated into the techniques of modern banking (such as letters of exchange), and carried out a gradual transformation of commerce within the French social system during the sixteenth century and thereafter.[19] Their activities expanded, diversified, and extended geographically to the entire realm, then beyond its borders, and finally to other continents.

The mutation of the French merchant bourgeoisie began slowly during the fifteenth and sixteenth centuries, emerging in the seventeenth and even more fully in the eighteenth century. The appearance of a new social elite set

Table 5.1   Characteristics of Wealthy *Alhazai*, Arranged by Level of Economic Activity

Group	Number of Merchants	Annual Revenues (CFA francs)	Mode of Acquisition	Type of Commerce	Geographic Scope	Access to Credit
1	4	More than 2 billion	Rapid and recent	Very diverse	Very extensive (global)	Easy
2	15–20	200 million to 2 billion	Varied	Less diverse, sometimes specialized	Niger, Nigeria, other African countries	Sometimes difficult, occasionally guaranteed by Group 1 member
3	About 50	50 million to 200 million	Slow and gradual	Hardly diverse, often in traditional businesses (cattle, cola nuts)	Niger, Nigeria, but mainly in Maradi region	Rarely obtainable unless guaranteed by wealthier *Alhazai*

in motion profound modifications in social relationships, prefiguring those of the industrial society to which it would give birth.

The evolution of the French bourgeoisie, very briefly traced, shows some resemblance to the changes now under way in African cities: after subordination at first to foreign commerce, local development occurs, followed by seizure of the national economy at the expense of other social groups. Still, though the evolution of the bourgeoisie at Maradi is similar to that in France, it nonetheless has its own distinctive characteristics.

For one thing, the relationship of patron (uban-gida) to servant (bara), emphasized repeatedly throughout this book, still plays a crucial role, and its social content is indivisible from its economic content. The relationship is created by an exchange, a trading of effort for assistance and protection, and it remains the basis of many economic activities.

The other key factor is the mechanism of inheritance, which governs the distribution of estates. An estate is divided among the direct descendants (sons and daughters) of a deceased merchant; in cases where they are very numerous, the Alhazai often being polygamous, the decedent's wealth is dissipated. Inheritance being controlled by Islamic law, it militates against the creation of merchant dynasties such as existed in Italy (in Florence under the Medicis, for example) or in France during the seventeenth and eighteenth centuries. The phenomenon of dispersion is very important in Hausa culture: the fortune of an Alhaji must be divided among his many heirs.[20] As a result, there is generally no continuity to an individual's business enterprise; it disintegrates upon the merchant's death.[21]

Nevertheless, in the Hausa commercial milieu it is useful to make a distinction between an Alhaji's estate and his succession. Agier notes that while the estate is closed and jurisdiction over it passes solely to an Alhaji's descendants, the succession is by contrast quite open: "His succession passes not along filial lines but along commercial lines, that is, his ties with those of his dependents who are eligible for future rewards (after, but also even before the death of the maigida); it is based upon his reputation and his business relationships—in brief, upon his position within the commercial/ social system."[22]

The commercial position of the deceased is therefore as much in contention as his estate. The succession gives rise to a competition or a jockeying within the rules of clientism, and this takes place entirely outside the framework of family relationship. Those clients who are linked to the deceased as successors rise quickly through the ranks of the commercial hierarchy; in some cases the winner even takes over the vacated position. The process is an important element in the continuing renewal of the social system, thereby manifesting its dynamic character.

However, the future survival of this distinction between inheritance proper and commercial succession is open to doubt, for it appears probable that despite customary and religious constraints, great merchant families are in the process of formation. Many *Alhazai* now bring their sons into their businesses so that their heirs will replace them when they die. If it continues in coming years, this trend will be very important.

It seems possible, too, that the relationship between *bara* and *uban-gida*, the notion of *arzikin mutane*, and the inheritance mechanism as it currently operates are all simply examples of resistance on the part of the traditional Hausa society to evolution in the direction of social models—in particular, that of capitalism—that exist today in the industrialized countries.

In modern Niger there exists a merchant capitalism very loyal to free enterprise. If it does not soon transform itself into industrial capitalism, it may nonetheless evolve in the direction of greater economic individualism at the expense of community ties, or indeed it may generate entirely new social relationships.

THE LIFE OF THE WORKING CLASS

Besides stimulating the emergence of a bourgeoisie, urban growth has shaped the working people who constitute the major share of the city's inhabitants. These people are usually employed precariously in what is known as the "informal" sector. At Maradi, the modern sector is still insufficiently developed to offer real employment possibilities to workers.

Working people's origins are essentially rural; in fact, many divide their time between farming during the growing season and working in town during the dry season. Some, however, have become more or less permanent residents of Maradi, especially since the drought plunged rural areas into crisis. Their numbers are considerable, as was indicated in the section on demographic growth in Chapter 1.

In addition to the sporadic availability of resources, the world of work at Maradi is characterized by a great diversity of material and ideological differences among workers and also by the persistence of productive relationships in which the economic aspects are not the sole determinants; social, familial, and religious structures play an important role.

Workers' Origins

Workers from Rural Areas

Migration has been occurring in the area around Maradi for a long time. A wave of seasonal immigration (during the dry season) took place every year during the groundnut-trading decades, when there were many jobs available at the vegetable oil mill, in the market, and with the traders themselves (loading, unloading, transporting, and so on). The migrants were usually from the countryside around Maradi, but some came from as far away as the Ader massif.

The rural crisis at the beginning of the 1970s provoked an acceleration of the exodus, extending it to the entire *département* of Maradi and making some of the moves permanent. Research in the region showed that the exodus resulted from a number of socioeconomic factors as well as from the grave problems the peasant community confronted (among these, the precariousness of food supplies and the weakness in farm incomes were important). For many rural dwellers, migration was a means to mitigate the insufficiency of resources available from agriculture.

Many migrants headed toward Nigeria, although cities such as Maradi, Zinder, or Niamey were also destinations, which helps to explain their demographic dynamism. Future migration will depend in large part upon the agricultural policies to be adopted by the government's planners; the most extreme situations have been identified by Raynaut:

[1] Either an agricultural policy will favor the satisfaction of the food needs of the entire rural population and will limit the exodus by promoting widespread adoption of techniques that are simple and accessible to the largest possible number of producers, and by providing security stocks at the farm level—strategies that will no doubt limit commercialization of farm products and will thus affect food supplies to the cities; or, [2] it will encourage the creation of a class of farmers practicing an agriculture with an elevated rate of productivity, capable of producing a surplus; this implies support to the most favored elements of the rural community and the gradual elimination of many small producers who will not be able to keep up with the increasing pace of technology. Under the latter policy, the surplus will flow into commercial channels, especially toward the towns. Another result will be an acceleration of the exodus and the appearance of long term migrations.[23]

In practice, intermediate solutions are certainly possible. Case studies carried out in numerous villages show that during the 1980s the exodus was usually temporary, of short duration—a few months, generally broken into several repeated stays—affecting agricultural production very little. However, in some cases migration was transformed into permanent settlement in Maradi, which benefited more and more from the integration of these rural arrivals. Whether the migration is temporary or permanent, migrants furnish a good part of the city's unskilled labor. The rest is provided by workers who arrived much earlier, or by their offspring.

Workers of Urban Origin

The city is the central congregating point for a population of workers who are truly upwardly mobile. As Leon says, "It is in the town and because of the town that the world of work takes shape, gains its mass, and acquires its own mentality."[24]

The social evolution of the past decade suggests that in a center such as Maradi there exists an urban population more and more detached from its original milieu. Quite a few workers have lived there for many years. These city dwellers generally hold steadier jobs than do the seasonal immigrants; over the years, they have acquired professional training and experience that has made them the most qualified workers.

Working Conditions in Maradi

In the city, there are many different kinds of work, creating a particularly heterogeneous social scene. Jean Copans emphasizes that, among categories of African workers, "their heterogeneity is neither abnormal nor temporary but structural, ingrained in the logic of the labor market. Of course, the basis of this heterogeneity lies in the contradictory as well as complementary relationships between town and country, the modalities of the rural exodus, and the support provided to the nonagricultural work force by the domestic or peasant sectors of the economy."[25]

Great diversity is one of the key traits of the workaday world now emerging in African cities. In Maradi, a city of modest size where the industrial sector scarcely exists as yet, they can best be analyzed by organizing them according to ownership of the means of production, whatever the level of capital; this distinguishes small local employers from workers as such.

Small Local Employers

The term *petit patronat local* (small local employers), refers globally to artisans who own their means of production. They are distinguishable by one characteristic in particular: economic independence.

"Independent" artisans. Within the mass of small manufacturers, these are usually masters of their own destiny by virtue of the amount of primary materials they keep in stock and by the finished products they hold in inventory. An examination of metal furniture making provides examples of workshop owners whose operations have achieved a size that justifies calling them true small entrepreneurs.

For example, Samaila Sodo learned welding from a European for whom he worked for about ten years.[26] Having completed his training, he found a position as a skilled laborer, at first with Sonara and later with other local firms. Gradually he was able to save a bit of money from his wages, which he used to buy a welding outfit and to set up his own shop. In addition to working on automobiles, he made furniture (chairs, tables, armoires, etc.).

As his shop achieved success, Samaila Sodo bought other equipment and added employees. In 1979, with an associate, he created a true small enterprise, a metal fabricating firm divided into two departments, furniture and automobile repairs. For this purpose he obtained a loan of 2 million

CFA francs from the World Bank. Today he has become a veritable small entrepreneur.

Members of traditional craft associations (*sana' a*) can also be counted among such "independent" artisans. Usually they have very limited material means and work either alone or with a few apprentices. The work is organized along traditional caste system lines, with the apprentice utterly dependent upon the owner. Most of these shops have very little business but do maintain their economic independence, inasmuch as they are not tied to a specific clientele.

"Dependent" craftsmen. A more numerous group contains artisans who are not truly independent. Rather, they are closely linked to and dependent upon the merchants, who are in a position to refuse work or provide it as they see fit. Such artisans (tailors, shoemakers, carpenters, masons, etc.) produce goods to order. The merchants then sell the finished products, either in town or further afield, through agents who are part of their commercial networks. The advantage to artisans from such cooperative arrangements is a guaranteed outlet for their production. The disadvantage is that the merchants force very strong competition among producers in order to obtain very low prices, which the producers, not wanting to risk the survival of their enterprises, are forced to accept for lack of alternative outlets. As a result, some of them are not much more than common laborers, despite owning their own means of production.

The Workers

The most numerous of all are the common workers, spread among the myriad workshops and the multiple branches that constitute the crafts, small manufacturing, microcommerce, and services. The advantage to them is steadiness of employment combined with regularity of income. Three groups of workers are readily identifiable: "mixed," salaried, and nonsalaried workers.

"Mixed" workers. These workers divide their time between farming during the growing season and urban work during the dry season. They are seasonal migrants who come to Maradi during several months each year. Usually, their employment is characterized by its instability; many work from day to day and are paid day rates or piece rates. The work itself is usually very simple (porterage, masonry, painting, etc.) and requires no special qualifications. Some, however, are able to find regular work in the informal or even the modern sector (at the vegetable oil mill, for instance).

Sani, from a village near Kornaka, is an example. Twenty-two years old, he first came to Maradi in 1984 with the intention of finding a job during the dry season. After two months of unemployment, he obtained an introduction to the head of a metal furniture shop, who offered him a job and taught him a simple task (painting furniture) at a pay rate of 8,000 CFA francs a month. Over the following six months, Sani performed slightly more complex tasks (metal cutting, attaching springs to bed frames) and received higher pay— 12,000 CFA francs a month. He hopes to learn welding next.

With the approval of his boss, Sani leaves his job each year before the rains begin and returns to his village to help his parents with work in the fields. As soon as the harvest is in, he returns to Maradi and resumes his work. According to Sani, the job in town allows him to help his parents, to whom he regularly sends money. For the short term, he will continue to divide his time between Maradi and the bush, but as soon as he has learned his trade, he will try to start his own shop.

The existence of these mixed workers, these worker-peasants, is not limited to Africa. The economic and social history of France recalls individuals who divided their time more or less equally between the cultivation of the soil and the exercise of an industrial occupation. For example, during the eighteenth century, the miners of Littry, Allevard, and Sainte-Marie-aux-Mines were also peasants. Similarly, in the region of Carcassonne, laborers abandoned the workshops during the three months consecrated to harvesting grapes and other crops.[27]

The links between such workers and the rural world are therefore very strong; they have only a partial involvement with the town. Their mobility is a fact of life, testifying to the instability of their situation: their frequent arrivals and departures are guided by a desire to find more numerous and better-paid job opportunities. Maradi's rate of demographic growth suggests, however, that during the past decade or so more and more of them have decided to stay in the city. The episodes of drought that regularly afflict the region and the resulting shortfalls in agricultural production are obviously connected to the change.

Salaried workers. Found in the modern sector of the economy, which includes industrial enterprises and government administration, salaried workers are relatively few in number.[28] Their situation is characterized by stable employment and regular income. They also receive more in the way of perquisites, including family allowances, social security, medical coverage, and retirement pay. This gives them privileged status among the working population.

Since the private sector is not very important in Maradi, the government of Niger, through the intermediary of the state-owned or mixed-ownership firms, has been the principal employer of this kind of labor.[29] By virtue of its policies of investment and industrialization, the government has played an essential role in the labor market, which it nevertheless controls very strictly. In Niger, as in African countries examined by Copans, "the government not only defines the conditions of recruitment and management of the labor force, it also manipulates and frustrates workers' demands and activities."[30] He adds that "in virtually all African countries, the labor unions are more or less integrated vertically within the state apparatus." This situation corresponds closely to that in Niger, where the sole labor organization, the Union

Syndicale des Travailleurs Nigériens (USTN), is an arm of the government. As a result, labor disputes are rare and easily controlled.

Nonsalaried workers. This group is an important segment of the labor market in African cities. In a small city such as Maradi, they are likely to form the majority, concentrated in small enterprises, small commerce, and services. Members of this group are often very young, their numbers large but fluctuating. There are many different kinds of such workers:

First, there are some who work more or less regularly; they are classed as nonsalaried because they lack access to the perquisites available to those in the modern sector (allowances, social security, etc.). Since their earnings are liable to be reduced for various reasons, such as a slowing of business, they cannot be compared with people who earn real salaries. For example, the skilled workers employed at garages or metal furniture workshops belong to this group. Their incomes are regular enough, and their jobs are relatively stable. They have acquired skills that can render them indispensable to the effective operation of the workshops.

Second, a multitude of apprentices constitute a labor force that is not paid at full value by employers. Their pay may even be nonexistent; certainly it is sporadic. The exploitation of apprentices is masked by the social pretense that some day they will be able to become entrepreneurs in turn. Alain Morice reports that the "system of apprenticeship is made possible by the maintenance of a social fabric that assures the authority of the elder over the younger. In the workshop, power is created through the establishment of personal links between the protagonists, links that invert the image of exploitation by making the apprentice the bearer of an obligation to his employer."[31] A bit later he adds, "The African apprentice does not sell himself freely, as does a proletarian; he is offered through a pseudo-market for labor controlled by cliental, parental, or marital relationships."

Apprentices are found in all branches of economic activity, including commerce. Just as there exists a powerful merchant bourgeoisie in Maradi, there exist also a crowd of small and very small merchants, among them a sort of commercial "proletariat," at the beck and call of merchants and civil servants. Thus, Amadou, who comes from Dan Mero, has a spot near a gasoline station during the day; at night, he moves his table to the entrance at one of the cinemas. Amadou does not own his merchandise (cigarettes, matches, hard candies, chocolates, cookies, sugar, cola nuts, tomato concentrate, bouillon cubes, dry-cell batteries, etc.). It is confided to him by a merchant who pays him weekly according to how much he has sold. Amadou's weekly earnings vary between 1,250 and 2,000 CFA francs.

Finally, part-time workers, usually very young, have no links to any particular employer. Their lack of qualifications and connection to an employer leaves these workers floating and their work unstable. Their activities vary according to opportunities to work, which they seek out in the construction business (as mason's helpers), transportation (loading and unloading), or in the market (running errands).

As this review shows, the world of work is extremely diverse; this makes it difficult to apprehend. Everywhere, in town or in the country, women and children are employed routinely. Women engage in small commerce, playing an important role by providing cooked foods, and also to an extent in weaving mats. As for the children, they are used from a very early age for family chores or simple work, and from age ten or twelve years many begin to work regularly. As an example, Salissou, who is thirteen years old, helps make clothing in a leather workshop. His father, who earns a very modest living, wants his son to work in order to supplement the family's resources. He has therefore bound his son over to the owner, who cares for the child and teaches him his craft, feeding him at midday and giving him 3,000 to 5,000 CFA francs each month. There are countless examples of this kind.

Conclusion

This quick review of Maradi's labor sector leads to the following question: does this social system, made up of workers and apprentices, constitute a proletariat in the sense understood in the West since its emergence during the nineteenth century?

Some authors do not hesitate to take a firm position on the subject. Claude Meillassoux speaks of an informal-sector proletariat: "Although not employed directly by owners of major capital, and although not stable enough to become unionized, this population nevertheless constitutes a proletariat for two reasons: (1) it performs work in the microcapitalist sector, generating profits directly or indirectly for capitalists, who (2) are thereby armed with surplus capital, the function of which is to keep pressure on the working proletariat and to cushion the cycles of employment and unemployment."[32]

This judgment is a bit hasty, at least if applied to a small city such as Maradi, which has no true industrial sector. There, most urban employment is furnished by the informal sector, in which work relationships are based largely upon social ties (clientage, consanguinity, or marriage) rather than purely economic ties (wages). Thus, many workers, particularly apprentices, are not able to "sell themselves freely as proletarians," to recall Morice's expression, because they are enmeshed in a complex system of social relations from which they cannot escape.

The idea of a proletariat implies the idea of wages. In Maradi, the concept of wages is very fluid, since payment can be irregular and can take multiple forms (by the piece, the day, the week, or the month); the low rates make these workers extremely dependent upon the price of food.

Finally, the informal sector lacks certain aspects normally associated with a proletariat. Its capacity to organize is practically nonexistent or very much dependent upon the state apparatus (as is also the case for workers in the modern sector), which thus controls workers' activities and movements. Moreover, class consciousness scarcely exists, leaving the working community very much divided as well as dependent upon a hierarchy in which the elders exercise authority over the young.

Thus, the concept of proletariat appears ill suited to a city such as Maradi, where social relationships are strongly rooted and guided by ancient social structures. The relationship between patron and servant (*uban-gida* and *bara*) still plays a key role in many activities, even though so transformed as to be scarcely recognizable at times.

Nevertheless, it is worth asking how long these ancient relationships will resist change, and whether that change will take place very soon— whether the economy will soon emphasize the individual at the expense of society. In that case, all these little apprentices and workers will be replaced by a true proletariat, and a wage-earning labor pool will supplant the complex traditional system that exists today.

NOTES

1. Samaria is a youth movement intended to give young people opportunities to meet and organize activities. Under supervision by local authorities, they also undertake various volunteer projects.

2. In contrast to Zinder, where many merchants had relatives involved in commerce during the precolonial period, at Maradi most of the *Alhazai* went into business on their own.

3. The concept of profit, clearly defined in the Hausa language, distinguishes between a monetary profit gained from a commercial transaction (*riba*), which is authorized by Muslim law, and the interest earned on a sum of money loaned out (*ribā*), which is forbidden.

4. In any case, most of the *Alhazai* can neither read nor write.

5. Many deals are done in cash, avoiding the banks altogether. According to bank employees, from time to time a merchant will come in carrying an enormous sum of money in a tin box.

6. The *Alhazai* practice confinement of women, a Muslim custom frequent in northern Nigeria but less widespread in the Maradi region, where women traditionally have had more autonomy (they are allowed to engage in commerce). This behavior, which is fairly new, may have its origins in the *Alhazai's* material prosperity.

7. Claude Raynaut, *Structures normatives et relations électives: étude d'une communauté villageoise haoussa* (Paris: Mouton, 1973).

8. The *Alhazai* also make gifts to *griots* to get them to sing praises of their generosity, in accordance with an ancient custom of Hausa society.

9. In 1978, at the finals of the championships in traditional wrestling held at Maradi, a rich *Alhaji* strode into the center of the arena to reward the two athletes. Upon returning to his seat, he reached into the pockets of his *boubou* and pulled out wads of banknotes, which he threw into the air, provoking a general tumult among the spectators.

10. The pilgrimage to Mecca, which an *Alhaji* may undertake several times during his life, often leads him to make special gifts (religious objects, etc.) upon his return. It is also an opportunity to do some business with items picked up during the trip.

11. For purposes of comparison, the government of Niger's budget was 94 billion CFA francs in 1982.

12. However, their activity is still centered on Niger and Nigeria.

13. His name has been changed.

14. He was one of the players in "the pea scandal" involving cowpea sales at artificial naira/CFA franc exchange rates (see Chapter 4).

15. *Alhaji* Oumarou's name has also been changed.

16. *Hadjia* is the Hausa honorific applied to a woman who has made the pilgrimage to Mecca—Translator.

17. *Alhaji* Maman is not his true name.

18. Chaunu and Gascon, *Histoire économique et sociale de la France*, Tome 1: *De 1450 a 1660*, Vol. 1: *L'Etat et la ville*.

19. In the Hausa country, certain modern banking practices were already known before the beginning of colonialism, thanks to Arab merchants; cf. Baier, *An Economic History of Central Niger*.

20. Only one case has come to hand in which the heirs of a deceased major merchant maintained the integrity of his fortune and kept his business in operation.

21. In a study of a village community, Polly Hill presents evidence that the inheritance rules act as an equalizing mechanism; she cites division of a rich man's lands, following his death, among his many descendants. Cf. her *Rural Hausa: A Village and a Setting* (Cambridge: Cambridge University Press, 1972).

22. Agier, "Commerce et sociabilité: les négociants soudanais du quartier Zongo de Lomé, (Togo)."

23. Raynaut, *Recherches multi-disciplinaires*.

24. E. Labrousse, P. Leon, P. Goubert, J. Bouvier, C. Carriere, and P. Harsin, *Histoire économique et sociale de la France*, Vol. 2: *Des derniers temps de l'âge seigneurial aux préludes de l'âge industriel (1660–1789)* (Paris: Presses Universitaires de France, 1970).

25. Jean Copans, "Classes ouvrières du Tiers-Monde," *Le Monde Diplomatique* (Paris), December 1982.

26. His name has been changed.

27. Labrousse et al., *Histoire économique*.

28. Salaried workers in the industrial sector, for example, total about 500 persons.

29. Under structural adjustment programs supported by the World Bank and other donors during the late 1980s, the government of Niger liquidated or privatized many state-owned firms in order to reduce the drain on the national budget caused by their chronic business losses. The number of jobs available in these firms thus declined sharply, leaving many workers unemployed— Translator.

30. Jean Copans, "En Afrique noire: un monde instable," *Le Monde Diplomatique* (Paris), December 1982.

31. Alain Morice, "Les travailleurs non-salariés en Afrique," *Le Monde Diplomatique* (Paris), December 1982.

32. Claude Meillassoux, "Paysans africains et travailleurs immigrés: de la surexploitation au génocide par la faim," in a special edition of *Tricontinental* entitled *La France contre l'Afrique* (Paris: Maspéro, 1981).

General Conclusions

The development of Maradi has set in motion profound disturbances to local social organization, creating distinct social groups and, between them, cleavages that have become deeper with the passage of time. The changes suggest the following question: Does Maradi now have social classes, in the Marxist sense of that term?

The idea of class, in the modern sense of the word, implies a level of industrialization that brings productive relationships to the fore, favoring the formation of groups based upon the antagonism between labor and capital; at its heart it implies an awareness of the antagonism, that is to say, a class consciousness.

Maradi is not yet an industrial city; its modern sector is at an early stage of development. The commercial sector and the informal sector provide most employment, and the only productive relationships exist within traditional social relationships. Relationships involving work extend deep into the social fabric, and the economic ties linking the owner of a workshop to an apprentice or an *Alhaji* to a street vendor are only as important as the affective and social ties that link them.

The emergence of a merchant class has thus not provided local society a vertical structure, as might have been expected; rather, the structure is pyramidal: social relationships are based upon ties of allegiance between a *bara*, or servant/client, and an *uban-gida*, or patron. A traditional social relationship has thus been revitalized within a modern commercial structure. The *Alhazai* have clients rather than employees.

Perhaps, as Jean-Jacques Beassou speculates, this clientist structure will help avoid class conflicts: "From the bottom to the top of the hierarchy, the social goal is the same; individual and mercantile success coexist within strong familial structures, justifying the position of the merchant class."[1] His observation underscores the impossibility of artificially separating the economic from the social, for in this society, social, familial, and religious ties function as productive relationships.

Will this system of social relationships persist? Conversations with *Alhazai*, with artisans, and with laborers in the tiniest workshops provide evidence that they are increasingly aware of the social differences separating them. It is probable that their social awareness will increase with time, parallel to the deepening of cleavages and the intensification of individualism. What is happening today is the birth of enterprises in which the economic is becoming more important than the social; if the newly appeared phenomenon of merchant dynasties takes hold, it will strengthen the trend, whereas at an earlier period the mechanism of inheritance produced a division of wealth among relatives, acting as a great equalizer, as Polly Hill showed in another context.[2]

It appears, however, that with respect to religion, a new social solidarity is being created, one that draws individuals together: Islam, even though it does not erase social differences, does bring together in a solidarity of same beliefs the *Alhaji*, the civil servant, the artisan, the table vendor, the laborer, the apprentice. It thus constitutes, with tradition, a brake on the establishment of new social relationships similar to those that exist in the West, where the economy is entirely detached from society. This still solid link between the economic and the social permits the merchant class to live in close proximity with the traditional system of values; it confers upon its members a popular respectability that the political class finds hard to attain.

LINKS BETWEEN THE MERCHANT AND POLITICAL CLASSES

Parallel to the emergence of the merchant bourgeoisie holding most of the economic power, the creation of an independent state has led to the emergence of a political and bureaucratic bourgeoisie controlling the legislative and regulatory power. Relations between the two groups have taken diverse forms since independence—sometimes close, sometimes conflicting.

For example, the *Alhazai* benefited from government support when Sonara and Copro-Niger were created, and from the national credit-issuing institutions, all of which helped them displace the economic agents put into place by the colonial administration. However, a bit later (beginning in 1968) they found themselves thrown into opposition to the state when it developed a large cooperative commercial sector and tried to organize the peasants.

The links between the merchant class and the political class are therefore fairly variable, ranging from total complicity (for example, the special authorizations accorded to merchants by the government for specific operations) to strong hostility (in the case of commerce in food products);

however, these swings remain within certain limits, the politicians becoming angry at the *Alhazai* because of their impact on the population but avoiding violent confrontations. This mixture of collusion and opposition between the two groups has been a marked trait of political life in Niger ever since independence.

Finally, the emergence of a merchant bourgeoisie in the context of its city, its region, and its country has a more general significance: the mechanisms of wealth accumulation by Sahelian merchants, and in fact merchants all over Africa, are no doubt very similar to those used by the *Alhazai* of Maradi.

NOTES

1. Jean-Jacques Beaussou, "Genèse d'une classe marchande au Niger: continuité ou rupture dans l'économie sociale," in Vol. 1 of *Entreprises et entrepreneurs en Afrique, XIXème et XXème siécle* (Paris: Harmattan, 1983), pp. 205–220.

2. Polly Hill, "Notes on the History of the Northern Katsina Tobacco Trade," *Studies in Rural Capitalism in West Africa*, African Studies Series 2 (Cambridge: Cambridge University Press, 1970).

Acronyms

AOF	Afrique Occidentale Française (French West Africa)
BCEAO	Banque Centrale des Etats de l'Afrique de l'Ouest (Central Bank of West African States)
BDRN	Banque de Développement de la République du Niger
BIAO	Banque Internationale de l'Afrique Occidentale
BNA	Bloc Nigérien d'Action
CEA	Commissariat à l'Energie Atomique (Atomic Energy Agency)
CFA	Communauté Financiére Africaine
CFAO	Compagnie Française de l'Afrique de l'Ouest
CFDT	Compagnie Française de Développement des Textiles
CNF	Compagnie du Niger Français
CSON	Conseil Supérieur d'Orientation Nationale (High Council for National Direction)
CSPN	Caisse de Stabilisation des Produits du Niger
FIDES	Fond d'Investissement pour le Développement Economique et Social (Investment Fund for Economic and Social Development)
GMV	groupement mutuel villageois (village cooperative)
IMF	International Monetary Fund
MNSD	Mouvement National pour la Société de Développement (National Movement for a Developing Society)
MSA	Mouvement Socialiste Africain
OCA	Office de Commercialisation Agricole
OCDN	Organisation Commune Dahomey-Niger (Dahomey-Niger Cooperative Organization)
OPVN	Office des Produits Vivriers du Niger (Food Products Office of Niger)
PPN	Partu Progressiste Nigerien (Niger Progressive Party)

RDA	Rassemblement Democratique Africain (African Democratic Assembly)
RVA	regroupement des villages animés (cooperative of active villages)
SAH	Société Africaine des Huiles (African Vegetable Oils Company)
SAPM	Société Algérienne des Pétroles Mory
SCOA	Société Commerciale de l'Ouest Africain
SNCP	Société Nigérienne des Cuirs et des Peaux (Niger Hides and Skins Company)
SNTN	Société Nationale des Transports du Niger
SOCOPAO	Société Commerciale des Ports d'Afrique de l'Ouest
Sonara	Société Nigérienne de Commercialisation de l'Arachide (Niger Groundnut Marketing Company)
Sonibri	Société Nigérienne de Briquetterie (Niger Brick Company)
Sonifac	Société Nigérienne de Fabrication de Couvertures (Niger Blanket Company)
Sonigec	Société Nigérienne du Gypse et de la Cire (Niger Gypsum and Wax Company)
Sonipal	Société Nigérienne de Production d'Allumettes (Niger Match Company)
Sonitan	Société Nigérienne de Tannierie
UCN	Union Commerciale du Niger
UDN	Union Démocratique Nigérienne
UMOA	Union Monétaire Ouest-Africaine (West African Monetary Union)
UNCC	Union Nigérienne de Crédit et de Coopération
UNIS	Union des Nigériens Indépendants et Sympathisants
UPN	Union Progressiste Nigérienne
USAID	US Agency for International Development
USTN	Union Syndicale des Travailleurs Nigériens

Bibliography to the English-Language Edition

Abadie, M. *La colonie du Niger (Afrique Centrale)*. Paris: Société d'éditions géographiques, 1927.

Agier, Michel. *Commerce et sociabilité: les négociants soudanais du quartier Zongo de Lomé (Togo)*. Collection mémoires, No. 99. Paris: ORSTOM, 1983.

Amselle, J. L. *Les négociants de la savanne: histoire et organisation sociale des kooroko du Mali*. Paris: Anthropos, 1977.

Bagayogo, I. "Emergence d'une bourgeoisie agraire au Mali: exemple des planteurs de la région de Bamako." Doctoral thesis, third cycle, Ecole des Hautes Etudes en Sciences Sociales, 1982.

Baier, S. "African Merchants in the Colonial Period: A History of Commerce in Damagaram (Central Niger), 1880–1960." Ph.D. dissertation, University of Wisconsin (Madison), 1974.

————. *An Economic History of Central Niger*. Oxford: Clarendon Press, 1980.

Baier, S., and Lovejoy, P. E. "The Desert Side Economy of the Central Sudan." *International Journal of African Historical Studies* 8, 4 (1975):551–581.

Bala Usman, U. "The Transformation of Katsina (1796–1903): The Overthrow of the Sarauta System and the Establishment and Evolution of the Emirate." Ph.D. dissertation, Ahmadu Bello University, 1974.

Barth, Heinrich. *Voyages et découvertes dans l'Afrique septentrionale et centrale pendant les années 1849 à 1855*. Translated from the German by P. Ithier. Paris: A. Bohné, 1860–1861.

Bashir, L. "The Politics of Industrialization in Kano: Industries, Incentives, and Indigenous Entrepreneurs, 1950–1980." Ph.D. dissertation, Boston University, 1983.

Beaussou, J. J. "Genèse d'une classe marchande au Niger: continuité ou rupture dans l'économie sociale." In *Entreprises et entrepreneurs en Afrique, XIXème et XXème siécle*. Paris: Harmattan, 1983.

Bredeloup, S. *Négociants au Long cours, Rôle moteur du commerce dans une région de Côte d'Ivoire*. Paris: Harmattan, 1989.

Centre National de la Recherche Scientifique. "La croissance urbaine en Afrique noire et à Madagascar." Colloquium of September 29 to October 2, 1970. Bordeaux: CEGET, n.d.

Charmes, J. "Les contradictions du développement du secteur non structuré." In *Secteur informel et petite production marchande dans les villes du Tiers-Monde*, *Revue Tiers-Monde* 21 (April-June 1980).

Chaunu, P., and Gascon, R. *Histoire économique et sociale de la France*. Tome 1, *De 1450 à 1660*, Vol. 1: *L'Etat et la ville*. Paris: Presses Universitaires de France, 1977.

Collins, J. D. "The Clandestine Movements of Groundnuts Across the Niger-Nigeria Boundary." *Revue Canadienne des Etudes Africaines* 10, 2 (1976):259–276.

Copans, J. "Classes ouvrières du Tiers-Monde." *Le Monde Diplomatique* 345 (December 1982).

————— "En Afrique noire: un monde instable." *Le Monde Diplomatique* 345 (December 1982).

—————. *Les marabouts de l'arachide: la confrérie mouride et les paysans du Sénégal*. Paris: Sycomore, 1980.

Dan Asabe, A. U. *Comparative Biographies of Selected Leaders of the Kano Commercial Establishment*. Kano, Nigeria: Department of History, Bayero University, 1989.

David, Philippe. "La geste du grand Kaura Assao." *Documents des Etudes Nigériennes* 17 (1967).

—————. "Maradi, l'ancien Etat et l'ancienne ville: site, population, histoire." *Documents des Etudes Nigériennes* 18 (1964).

Doumesche, H., Nicolas, G., and Dan Mouche, M. "Etude socio-économique de deux villages hausa." *Documents des Etudes Nigériennes* 22.

Dunbar, R. A. "Damagaram (Zinder, Niger), 1812–1906: The History of a Central Sudanic Kingdom." Ph.D. dissertation, University of California (Los Angeles), 1970.

Faure, Y. A., and Medard, J. F. *Etat et bourgeoisie en Côte d'Ivoire*. Paris: Karthala, 1981.

Fourage, G. and Vanoye, J. *Le passé du Niger*. Studies and documents published in Vol. 1, *De l'antiquité à la pénétration coloniale*, and Vol. 2, *Régions et économie au XIXème siècle*. Niamey: Centre Pédagogique, 1972 and 1973.

Foureau, F. "D'Alger au Congo par le Tchad." *Documents scientifiques de la mission saharienne: mission Foureau-Lamy*. Paris: Mason, 1903.

Fuglestad, F. *A History of Niger, 1850–1960*. African Studies Series 41. Cambridge: Cambridge University Press, 1983.

Grégoire, E. "Accumulation marchande et propagation de l'Islam en milieu urbain: le cas de Maradi (Niger)." *Islam et Sociétés au Sud du Sahara*, forthcoming.

—————. "L'artisanat dans la ville de Maradi." Republic of Niger: Ministry of Plan, Service Départemental, 1979.

————— "Les chemins de la contrebande: étude de réseaux commerciaux en pays haoussa." *Cahiers d'Etudes Africaines*, forthcoming.

—————. "Développement urbain et accumulation marchande: les *Alhazai* de Maradi (Niger)." Doctoral thesis, third cycle, University of Bordeaux III, 1983.

—————. *Etude socio-économique du village de Gourjae (département de Maradi, Niger)*. Bordeaux: University of Bordeaux II, 1980.

────── "Formation d'une capitalisme africain: les *Alhazai* de Kano." *La Dimension Economique*. Collection Colloques et Séminaires. Paris: ORSTOM, 1990.

──────. "Les perspectives d'accumulation dans la petite industrie de transformation: l'exemple de la menuiserie métallique à Maradi (Niger)." *Cahiers d'Etudes Africaines* 21, 1-3 (1981–1983). Special issue entitled *Villes africaines au microscope*.

Grégoire, E., and Amselle, J. L. "Complicités et conflits entre bourgeoisies d'Etat et d'affaires au Mali et au Niger." *L'Etat contemporain en Afrique*. Paris: Harmattan, 1987.

Grégoire, Emmanuel, and Raynaut, Claude. *Présentation générale du département de Maradi*. Bordeaux: University of Bordeaux II, 1980.

Hamani, D. M. "Histoire." *Atlas du Niger, Les atlas Jeune Afrique*. Paris: Jeune Afrique, 1980.

Herry, C. *Croissance urbaine et santé à Maradi (Niger): Caracteristiques démographiques, phénomènes migratoires*. Bordeaux: Editions du GRID, 1990.

Hill, Polly. "Landlords and Brokers: A West African Trading System (with a Note on Kumasi Butchers)." *Cahiers d'Etudes Africaines* 23:349–366.

──────. "Notes on the History of the Northern Katsina Tobacco Trade." In *Studies in Rural Capitalism in West Africa*. African Studies Series 2. Cambridge: Cambridge University Press, 1970.

──────. *Rural Hausa: A Village and a Setting*. Cambridge: Cambridge University Press, 1972.

Hogendorn, J. S. *Nigerian Groundnut Exports: Origin and Early Development*. Zaria, Nigeria: Ahmadu Bello University Press and Oxford University Press, 1978.

Hopkins, A. G. *An Economic History of West Africa*. New York: Columbia University Press, 1973.

Hugon, P. "Secteur informel et petite production marchande dans les villes du Tiers-Monde." *Revue Tiers-Monde* 21 (April-June 1980).

──────. "Les petites activités marchandes dans les espaces urbains africains: essai de typologie." *Revue Tiers-Monde* 21 (April-June 1980).

Iliffe, J. *The Emergence of African Capitalism*. London: Macmillan, 1983.

Janvier, J. "Autour des missions Voulet-Chanoine en Afrique Occidentale." *Présence Africaine* 22 (October-November 1958).

Joalland, D. *Le drame de Dan Kori*. Paris: Argo, 1931.

Johnson, Marion. "Calico Caravans: The Tripoli-Kano Trade After 1880." *Journal of African History* 17 (1976).

Kennedy, P. *African Capitalism: The Struggle for Ascendancy*. Cambridge: Cambridge University Press, 1988.

Labazée, P. *Entreprises et entrepreneurs au Burkina Faso*. Paris: Harmattan, 1988.

Labrousse, E., Leon, P., Goubert, P., Bouvier, J., Carriere, C., and Harsin, P. *Histoire économique et sociale de la France*, Vol. 2: *Des derniers temps de l'âge seigneurial aux préludes de l'âge industriel (1660–1789)*. Paris: Presses Universitaires de France, 1970.

Lovejoy, P. and E. *Caravans of Cola: The Hausa Cola Trade, 1700–1900*. Zaria, Nigeria: Ahmadu Bello University Press, 1980.

────── "The Kamberin Beriberi: The Formation of a Specialized Group of Hausa Kola Traders in the Nineteenth Century." *Journal of African History* 14, 4 (1973).

Meillassoux, C. Introduction. In *The Development of Indigenous Trade and Markets in*

West Africa, International African Institute, ed. Oxford: Oxford University Press, 1971.

———. "Paysans africains et travailleurs immigrés: de la surexploitation au génocide par la faim." Special issue, *La France contre l'Afrique, Tricontinental* 1. Paris: Maspero, 1981.

Morice, A. "Les travailleurs non-salariés en Afrique." *Le Monde Diplomatique* 345 (December 1982).

Nicolas, G. *Don rituel et échange marchand dans une société sahelienne*. Paris: Institut d'éthnologie, 1986.

———. "Etudes des marchés en pays haoussa." *Documents ethnographiques*. Bordeaux: 1964.

———. "Une forme atténuée du potlatch en pays hausa (République du Niger)." *Economies et Sociétés* 2 (1967).

———. "Le Nord est destiné à jouer un rôle majeur." *Le Monde*, October 18, 1981.

———. "La pratique traditionelle du crédit au sein d'une société sub-saharienne (Vallée de Maradi, Niger)." *Cultures et développement*. Louvain: Catholic University, 1974.

———. "Processus d'approvisionnement vivrier d'une ville de Savane Maradi (Niger)". *Travaux et documents de géographie tropicale*. Bordeaux: CEGET, 1972.

———. "Remarques sur divers facteurs socio-économiques de la famine au sein d'une société subsaharienne." In *Drought in Africa*. London: International African Institute, 1977.

Niger, Republic of. *Annuaire statistique 1978–1979*. Ministry of Plan, Office of Statistics and National Accounts.

———. *Plan quinquennal de développement économique et social, 1979–1983*. Ministry of Plan.

———. *Recensement général de la population 1977: résultats provisoires*. Ministry of Plan, 1978.

———. *Situation d'ensemble et suivi des deux premières années du Plan*. Ministry of Plan, 1981.

Pehaut, Y. *L'arachide au Niger*. Centre d'Etudes d'Afrique Noire of the Institut d'Etudes Politiques, University of Bordeaux. Bordeaux: A. Pedone, 1970.

Perie, J. "Notes historiques sur la région de Maradi." Bulletin of IFAN 1 (1939).

Raynaut, Claude. "Le cas de la région de Maradi." In *Sécheresses et famines du Sahel*, ed. J. Copans. Paris: Maspero, 1975.

———. *Le développement de la région au village*. Bordeaux: Editions du GRID, 1988.

———. *Recherches multi-disciplinaires sur la région de Maradi: rapport de synthèse*. Bordeaux: University of Bordeaux II, 1980.

———. *Structures normatives et relations électives: étude d'une communauté villageoise haoussa*. Paris: Mouton, 1973.

———. "Trente ans d'indépendance: Repères et tendances." *Politiques Africaines* 33 (1990).

Rega, D. "Les sociétés commerciales françaises en Afrique, ou les tribulations d'un impérialisme mercantile." Special issue, *La France contre l'Afrique, Tricontinental* 1. Paris: Maspéro, 1981.

Robinet, A. M. "La chèvre rousse de Maradi: son exploitation et sa place dans l'économie de l'élevage de la République du Niger." *Revue d'élevage et de médicine vétérinaire des pays tropicaux*.

Rocheteau, G. *Pouvoir financier et indépendance économique en Afrique noire: le cas de Sénégal.* Paris: Karthala, 1981.

Rolland, J. F. *Le Grand Capitaine: un aventurier inconnu de l'épopée coloniale.* Paris: Grasset, 1976.

Sabo, Nassirou. *Perspectives d'évolution des activités commerciales vers des activités directement productives à Maradi (Niger).* Algiers: Institute des Techniques de Planification et d'Economie Appliquée, 1978.

Sa'id, H. I. "Revolution and Reaction: The Fulani Jihad in Kano and Its Aftermath, 1807–1919." Ph.D. dissertation, University of Michigan, 1978.

Salifou, A. "Le Damagaram ou sultanat de Zinder au XIXème siècle." *Documents des Etudes Nigériennes* 27 (1971).

———— "Malam Yaroh, un grand négociant du Soudan Central à la fin du XIXème siècle." *Journal de la Société des Africanistes* 42 (1972):7–27.

Sar, M. "Louga: la ville et sa région." Doctoral thesis, third cycle, University of Dakar.

Sawadogo, P. "Enquête sur les nomades refoulés par la sécheresse, zones de Maradi et Dakoro, Niger." Dakar: Training for the Environment Program, IDEP-UNEP-SIDA, 1974.

Seny, B. "Maradi, capitale économique et grand centre commercial." *Le Sahel Hebdomadaire,* August 25 and September 1, 1975.

Sere de Rivières, E. *Histoire du Niger.* Paris: Berger-Levrault, 1965.

————. *Le Niger.* Paris: Société d'Editions Géographiques Maritimes et Coloniales, 1952.

Shenton, R. *The Development of Capitalism in Northern Nigeria.* London: James Currey, 1986.

Sidikou, Harouna H. "Niamey: étude de géographie socio-urbaine." Doctoral thesis, University of Haute-Normandie (Rouen), 1980.

Smith, M. G. "A Hausa Kingdom: Maradi Under Dan Baskore, 1854–1875." In *West African Kingdoms in the Nineteenth Century,* ed. Daryll Forde and P. M. Kaberry. Oxford: Oxford University Press, 1967.

Spittler, G. "Migrations rurales et développement économique: exemple du canton de Tibiri (département de Maradi)." Mimeograph, 1970.

———— "Traders in Rural Hausaland." Bulletin of IFAN, Series B, 2, 39 (1977).

Suret-Canale, J. *Afrique noire occidentale et centrale.* Paris: Editions Sociales, 1966.

Tahir, I. "Scholars, Sufis, Saints and Capitalism in Kano, 1904–1974." Ph.D. dissertation, Cambridge University, 1975.

Tilho, J. *Documents scientifiques de la mission Tilho (1906–1909).* Vol. 2. Paris, 1910–1914.

Urvoy, Y. *Histoire des populations du Soudan Central (Colonie du Niger).* Publications of the Comité d'Etudes Historiques et Scientifiques de l'AOF. Series A, No. 5. Paris: Larose, 1936.

Usman, Usufu Bala. "The Transformation of Katsina (1796–1903): The Overthrow of the Sarauta System and the Establishment and Evolution of the Emirate." Ph.D. dissertation, Ahmadu Bello University, 1974.

Yenikoye, A. A. "La justice du droit local." National Archive, Republic of Niger.

Index

Abuja, Nigeria, 25

Afrique Occidentale Française (AOF), 43

Agadez, Niger, population growth in, 19

Agriculture for cash and profit, 146

Aïr mountains, Niger. *See* Uranium mining

Alhazai (singular, *Alhaji*): biographical sketches of (using pseudonyms in some cases): Ali, 112; Boubakar, 79–80, 149; Daouda, 53, 59, 64, 82n, 154; Gambo Maigoro, 59–60, 64, 86; Habou, 150–152; Malam Nasaru, 47; Maman, 154–155; Maman dan Dano, 58, 106; Moussa, 106–107, 111; Oumarou, 153; Ousmane, 63, 74, 95, 154; Saley, 112; Seydou, 130. Defined and described, 2; economic strategies of, 150–155; inheritance and succession among, 157; listed, 64, 123; as a social class, 143–150; tensions with political leaders, 3, 100, 168–169

Anna tribe, 31–32

Apprentices and apprenticeship, 135–137, 163–165

Arlit. *See* Uranium mining

Artisans, 134–138, 160–164. *See also* *Sana'a*

Arzikin mutane (richness in men), 2, 54, 64, 146, 147, 158

Babangida, Ibrahim, xi, 25

Banco (mud brick), 20, 54

Banque Centrale des Etats de l'Afrique de l'Ouest (BCEAO), xiii

Banque de Développement de la République du Niger, 74, 107, 129, 145, 151, 152

Banque Internationale de l'Afrique Occidentale (BIAO), 107, 145

Bara (dependent; plural, *barori*) and *uban-gida* (master) relationship, 58, 106, 145, 150; contrasted with apprenticeship, 136; defined, 54; as an element in *arzikin mutane*, 148; persistence and change in, 157–158, 165, 167

Barki, 31–32

Barth, Heinrich, 9

Benin, Republic of, 129, 150

Beri-Beri tribe, 13

Biafran war, 24, 25, 68, 78, 102, 106, 113, 123, 144, 149, 151. *See also* Nigeria, Federal Republic of

Bornou, empire of, 6, 8, 13, 37

Bourgeoisie, 2, 3; *Alhazai* as merchant, 103, 143–158; informal workers as potential, 163; links between political and merchant, 100, 168–169; political, 65

About the Book, Author, and Translator

The West African town of Maradi, capital of a prestigious nineteenth century Hausa chiefdom, became a trading center during the colonial period, and after Niger's independence in 1960, its prosperity and growth accelerated. Maradi's population increase (from 9,000 inhabitants in 1954 to nearly 100,000 by 1986) was accompanied by rapid social change, including the emergence of a rich business class known as the *Alhazai*, men steeped in the values of Islam but skilled in merchant capitalism. *Alhazai* is the plural of the Hausa honorific *Alhaji*, accorded to any Moslem who has made the pilgrimage to Mecca. Highly esteemed in Niger, the *Alhazai* proudly bear the title as a symbol of their economic success.

This book traces the history of Maradi and the accession to power and prestige of the *Alhazai*: When and how did they acquire their wealth? Why do they hold such a privileged place in local society? How do they conduct their business and are they motivated solely by profit? How do they interact with other participants in the economy and society? Answers to these questions provide a glimpse of social change in the making, as traditional and modern influences merge.

EMMANEL GRÉGOIRE obtained a masters degree in economics at the University of Paris I and a doctorate in tropical geography at the University of Bordeaux III. Currently engaged in research at the Centre National de la Recherche Scientifique (CRNS) in Paris, he is also affiliated with the Laboratoire de Sociologie et Géographie Africaines.

Dr. Grégoire's recent monographs and articles have focused on Hausa economic and business activity, primarily in Niger but also in Nigeria. He has visited Maradi and other Hausa communities repeatedly since 1977.

BENJAMIN H. HARDY, translator and editor, earned a Ph.D. in political science at the University of Chicago. A former diplomat and banker, he is a consultant on economic development in French-speaking West Africa.